Praise for *The Thinking Life*

"Being highly educated and extraordinarily decorated does not necessarily translate into good thinking. But if a Nobel Prize were awarded for gracious self-control, Professor Forni would be the proper judge. As with *Choosing Civility* and *The Civility Solution, The Thinking Life* serves well to refine even the most intransigent of us. Having just finished the book, I growled at my college-age daughter when she announced that her friends would visit our home late this evening. Then it immediately dawned on me that I was guilty of disobeying Professor Forni's thoughtful guidelines. Fortunately, my heartfelt apology was accepted. And for penance, I promise to think first next time."

—PETER AGRE, WINNER OF THE 2003 NOBEL PRIZE IN CHEMISTRY, PROFESSOR AT JOHNS HOPKINS BLOOMBERG SCHOOL OF PUBLIC HEALTH

THE THINKING LIFE

How to Thrive in
the Age of Distraction

P. M. Forni

ST. MARTIN'S PRESS
NEW YORK

www.stmartins.com

Library of Congress Cataloging-in-Publication Data

Forni, Pier Massimo.
    The thinking life : how to thrive in the age of distraction / P. M. Forni. — 1st ed.
      p. cm.
    ISBN 978-0-312-62571-9
  1. Thought and thinking.   2. Conduct of life.   3. Success.   I. Title.
II. Title: How to thrive in the age of distraction.
    BJ1595.F645 2011
    153.4'2—dc23

                                               2011019816

First Edition: September 2011

10 9 8 7 6 5 4 3 2 1

For Virginia, always

A Note of Thanks

To Christie Toribara and her family, Crystal Guenguerich, Claire Davis, Beth Holloway, William Leeb, Lucia Bosi, Dr. Stephen Reich, Lisa DiMona, Michael Flamini, Vicki Lame, Tobias Steed, Chris Aldrich, Tania Zampini, and Virginia Forni.

Thanks also to *One*, the magazine of the Carey Business School at Johns Hopkins University: A small fragment of this book appeared in its Spring/Summer 2010 issue.

P.M.F.
Towson, Maryland, April 2011

Contents

Contents

OURS IS AN AGE OF DISTRACTION. THE BACKGROUND OF OUR LIVES IS THE WHITE NOISE OF INCONSEQUENTIAL TELEVISION PROGRAMS, POMPOUS PUNDITS, SHRILL TALKBACK CALLERS, TEN-SECOND NEWS GRABS, AND THE CULT OF CELEBRITY. IN THIS ENVIRONMENT, THE NEED FOR CONTEMPLATION AND SOME INTROSPECTION BECOMES COMPELLING; A TIME TO STOP AND THINK; TO MAKE OUR WAY, GUIDED BY A MORAL COMPASS, A BEARING THAT DIVINES OUR BEST INSTINCTS.

—Paul Keating

THERE'S SOMETHING TO BE SAID
FOR SITTING STILL AND LETTING THINGS COME CLEAR,
THE WAY MORNING FOG BURNS OFF THE LAKE.

—George Witte

Preface

When the idea of writing a book that would rediscover the merits of the thinking life was still coalescing in my mind, one day I jotted down a couple of paragraphs with what, in essence, was the rationale behind the project. Quite uncharacteristically, those paragraphs were in the form of a report by a visitor to Earth from another galaxy. Having put them aside while I considered other projects, I had half forgotten them when I found them in a binder's pocket.

As the first week of my mission on Earth comes to a close, I must report a puzzling find. You remember that in a previous message I described the ability that all humans have to silently converse within their own selves. This internal conversation, which they call "thinking," allows them to take stock of the world around them and to plan their most suitable ways of dealing with it. If there is something that I could determine for sure about life on Earth, it is that happiness is the most coveted good, and that it is a by-product of the good life. You will then fully understand the importance of thinking when I tell you that it is virtually impossible to build a good life without the foundation of good thinking. What has been puzzling me is the cavalier way in which humans use such a core faculty. Any intergalactic visitor would be as struck as I am by their overindulging in thought-avoidance. The amount of their time spent in serious thinking does not even get close to that spent in mindless entertainment and the exchange of unnecessary information. From lack of thoughtful awareness of any situation in which they find themselves to the failure to prepare for adversity, inadequate thinking is without a doubt the number one cause of their grief and sorrow.

Even to a novice student of the human experience it becomes immediately apparent that good thinking is the necessary prelude to making good decisions. Training their children in it has to be a primary concern for human parents, you would think. Well, it is not. Does such training occupy a prominent position in the schools' curricula? It does not. And so good thinking fails to become second nature. On account of lack of thinking humans keep arriving unprepared to the crossroads of their lives where they must make decisions upon which the quality of their remaining time on Earth depends. In sum: A distinctive human character is the inclination to relentlessly pursue the trivial. That makes them waste an enormous amount of time and energy that would be better spent on matters of consequence. It is heartbreaking indeed to witness their unwitting sabotage of their own lives—because this is what their avoidance of serious thinking amounts to. I wonder what it is going to take for them to realize how crucial this issue is and to start a serious effort to reform their ways.

Respectfully submitted.

Now, I am not one who believes that when nobody is looking, extraterrestrial spaceships make scheduled stops in Paramus, New Jersey. In fact, I'm not even a science fiction fan. However, I know that a familiar landscape often escapes attention. It is the eyes of the stranger that see what remains unnoticeable under the varnish of the ordinary. In this case, the stranger was the extragalactic visitor who is struck by the fact that humans don't seem to realize they are not thinking nearly as much as they should. My challenge with this book is to make a few suggestions about changing that situation. I want to get as many people as possible to get serious about serious thinking.

In this age that has made distraction a way of life, the essence of my message could not be simpler: Think if you wish to thrive. In conveying it, I have enlisted some of the most influential thinkers from antiquity, such as Aristotle, Epictetus, Plato, and Marcus Aurelius. Being the product of an education that placed emphasis on the classics, I am at ease in their presence and enjoy pointing out all that in their thinking is relevant to our lives today. The essential features of human life have not changed in the last twenty-five hundred years, and the eloquent wisdom Athens and Rome have bequeathed us is still eminently applicable. Why reinvent the wheel when somebody is handing you a well-crafted and perfectly functioning one? This book will acquaint—or reacquaint—you with the basic and the best in thinking habits and thinking skills. Ultimately, the good life is the thinking life. If you want to reach its sunny shores, you'd better rediscover the causeways of thinking. It is by

Introduction
Thinking Seriously About Serious Thinking

BY THE BEGINNING OF 2009, THE AVERAGE AMERICAN CELL PHONE USER WAS SENDING OR RECEIVING NEARLY 400 TEXTS A MONTH, MORE THAN A FOURFOLD INCREASE FROM 2006. THE AVERAGE AMERICAN TEEN WAS SENDING OR RECEIVING A MIND-BOGGLING 2,272 TEXTS A MONTH. WORLDWIDE, WELL OVER TWO TRILLION TEXT MESSAGES ZIP BETWEEN MOBILE PHONES EVERY YEAR, FAR OUTSTRIPPING THE NUMBER OF VOICE CALLS. . . . IT'S OFTEN ASSUMED THAT THE TIME WE DEVOTE TO THE NET COMES OUT OF THE TIME WE WOULD OTHERWISE SPEND WATCHING TV. BUT STATISTICS SUGGEST OTHERWISE. MOST STUDIES OF MEDIA ACTIVITY INDICATE THAT AS NET USE HAS GONE UP, TELEVISION VIEWING HAS EITHER HELD STEADY OR INCREASED.
—*Nicholas Carr*

AREN'T A SOCIETY'S COMPETITIVENESS AND ITS PROSPECTS FOR A BETTER FUTURE ROOTED IN MORE THAN SHEER TECHNOLOGY? ISN'T HOW WELL WE USE THE DEVICES AS CRUCIAL AS HOW FAST THEY ARE? WILL PURSUING MORE AND MORE DIGITAL CONNECTEDNESS MAKE US SMARTER AND MORE CREATIVE? WILL IT HELP US UNDERSTAND ONE ANOTHER BETTER? WHEN WE'RE ALL HYPERCONNECTED, WILL OUR FAMILIES AND COMMUNITIES BE STRONGER? WILL WE BUILD BETTER ORGANIZATIONS AND

LEAD MORE PROSPEROUS LIVES? MOST IMPORTANT, CAN WE AC-
COMPLISH ANY OF THESE LOFTY GOALS IF WE CONTINUE DE-
VOTING ALL OUR ENERGY TO ELIMINATING THE VERY THING
WE NEED MOST TO ACHIEVE THEM IN THE FIRST PLACE—SOME
SPACE BETWEEN TASKS, RESPITES, STOPPING PLACES FOR THE
MIND?

—William Powers

A CRISIS OF CONCENTRATION

In late July 2008, as the race for the White House was fast approaching its homestretch, an utterly exhausted candidate Obama
flew to Europe on a multi-nation journey meant to invigorate his
credibility as a statesman. As he met with Tory leader David
Cameron in London, an ABC News live boom microphone picked
up the private and informal conversation, which then became
available to a world that was only too happy to eavesdrop. In it,
Mr. Cameron expressed concern about his American visitor's
punishing work regimen. After mentioning an upcoming short
August break, Mr. Obama shifted focus from lack of downtime
to lack of thinking time:

> But I agree with you that somebody, somebody who had
> worked in the White House who—not Clinton himself,
> but somebody who had been close to the process—said
> that, should we be successful, that actually the most im-
> portant thing you need to do is to have big chunks of time
> during the day when all you're doing is thinking.

While casting a glance toward his possible future, the candidate who would be president stressed the need for a president to set aside for thinking not just some time, but rather "big chunks of time." Letting oneself be swept along by the tidal wave of busyness was one of the worst things a president could do. "You start making mistakes, or you lose the big picture," Mr. Obama observed. Making good decisions was at the core of good politics, and good decisions were the result of good thinking, the two leaders agreed. One can't help wondering if former candidate Obama does set aside big chunks of thinking time as a resident of 1600 Pennsylvania Avenue. Of course, making—and keeping—appointments with your brain is beneficial not only to presidents but to all of us. Good thinking, however, doesn't just happen; it is the result of a personal commitment.

During the first decade of the new millennium, the digital media have changed the way we live. Every day, we spend most of our time doing things that our parents and grandparents not only did not do, but also could not even have imagined. Unfortunately, deep thinking is often the illustrious casualty in the digital revolution. As the most comprehensive encyclopedia ever assembled, the Internet yields serious and complex content. But we know that it is also a provider of mind-numbing distraction. The idea that communication is an intrinsically good thing seems to pervade our culture with the power of a self-evident truth. Hence—at least in part—the inordinate amount of time we spend online. That is unfortunate, because as we value the act of communicating, the value of what we are communicating becomes almost irrelevant. We have only a limited number of waking hours in our days. Time wasted online will never be graciously returned to us by benevolent Internet elves. It is bizarre how many of us have been time-profligate engaging in frivolous searches or retooling our images on social media, all the while neglecting to set aside even a few minutes to do some serious thinking. True, insight can travel by Twitter, but there is no substitute for uninterrupted reflection and introspection—not if we want to discover who we really are, check if we are true to our own values, learn from our mistakes, and plan our future. A lot of what goes online is technology-driven. We often communicate because we can, not because we need to. As we do so, we forget that the shape of our lives depends on what we make time for as we go through it. No, cyber-loitering does not qualify as thinking, and no, we cannot truly thrive without engaging in real thinking. That is why we must rediscover the very wise notion that communicating is only as good as what is being communicated. We must acquire the habit of consciously separating what's important from what is not and allocate our time accordingly. Norman Cousins said, "We in America have everything we need except the most important thing of all—time to think and the habit of thought." The statement may be hyperbolic, but it underscores a real problem with our current way of life. Only through bypassing the ever-present temptation to divert and amuse ourselves can we take the first, crucial step toward an engaged and rewarding life.

Google making us stupid?" That question happens to be the title of a seminal essay by Nicholas Carr, whose answer was a resounding "Yes" and who subsequently enshrined his "Yes" in a compelling monograph called *The Shallows*. Still, it may take years to fully qualify that "Yes." In the meantime, we can't go wrong by rediscovering and embracing serious thinking as a defense against a culture of distraction. Today we live with the feeling that there is too much life both physical and digital out there for our limited brainpower to sort out and absorb. The fast pace of innovation in technology often sends us scrambling to learn new skills in a world that appears more dauntingly complex every day. This complexity is matched by an equally daunting dearth of absolutes. For many of us, the only certainty we can rely on is that there are no certainties. This skepticism is not only unfortunate but also unwarranted. In reality, when it comes to what really counts, the age of Google is in perfect agreement with the age of Socrates. What constitutes a good life has not been a mystery for more than two thousand years. The good life is a life nurtured by a healthy sense of self-worth, brightened by a positive outlook, warmed by a loving family and loyal friends, grounded in congenial and challenging work, and made meaningful by an involvement in something larger than ourselves. We also know for sure that happiness is a by-product of the good life and the good life is a by-product of good thinking. Becoming a good thinker, then, is a prerequisite to achieving what all human beings want—in Sigmund Freud's words: "to become happy and to remain so." By "thinker," I do not mean a full-time philosopher, but rather anyone whose good thinking habits are part of his or her daily being in the world. "The life which is unexamined is not worth living," Socrates is famously said to have said. We may or may not be ready to endorse to the letter the powerful statement of a heroic thinker who chose to die to remain faithful to his principles. It is, however, difficult to quibble with his advocacy of submitting life to the scrutiny of reason. That is how good judgment comes into being. Any life habitually lacking this scrutiny is incomplete and unsafe. Yet we seek to spare ourselves the trouble of thinking as much as we can. We have literally made an art of it. The multibillion-dollar entertainment industry of our time is essentially built upon humanity's addiction to thought avoidance.

Choosing to live the thinking life, the challenge of this book, entails making a comprehensive commitment to the active life of the mind. When you choose the thinking life, you:

- Think first. Before saying or doing anything, you stop and think about the best ways at your disposal and about the likely consequences of your actions.

- Make paying attention your default mode of being in the world.

- Reduce substantially the time you devote to trivial distractions.

- Invest time in serious, uninterrupted introspection and reflection.

In this book on thinking, what I usually have in mind is critical thinking, the kind that is rational, informed, purposeful, and

1
Why You Don't Think and Why You Should

HEADS DOWN, WE ARE ALLOWING OURSELVES TO BE EVER-MORE
ENTRANCED BY THE UNSIFTED TRIVIA OF LIFE.

—*Maggie Jackson*

DOING WHAT IS OF
THE ESSENCE

They took their name from the Stoa Poikile, the famous painted porch in the heart of Athens where Zeno, their founder, philosophized. A Greek slave and a Roman emperor were two of the most influential among them. And in more than two thousand years of Western thought, you will not easily find more effective principles and strategies with which to face life's challenges than the ones they bequeathed us. I am talking about Stoicism, a school of thinking that flourished in Greece and Rome between the last three centuries BCE and the first two CE. The Stoics maintained that temperance in all things human and benevolence toward all people are part of the natural and rational order of things. Conforming to this order entails living a life of virtue, which is the only kind leading to happiness. We are the ones who make our own lives good or bad through the workings of our own thoughts. In other words, life is what the inclinations of the mind make it. A self-help author of our day might say, "Attitude is all." Since we have control—at least some—over our attitude, this is a comforting message, but of course it also saddles us with responsibility. Ultimately the Stoics say, "Life is up to us."

The Stoics did not disdain to address the ordinary and practical aspects of life. In his intellectual autobiography, which is at the same time a guide to the good life, Marcus Aurelius (121–180 CE), the emperor who fell in love with philosophy, wrote about everyday life topics such as learning from mistakes, minding your own business, and controlling anger. He also considered the wisdom of keeping the number of one's commitments as low as reasonably possible: "Is it not better simply to do what is necessary and no more, to limit yourself to what reason demands of a social animal and precisely in the manner reason dictates? This adds to the happiness of doing a few things the satisfaction of having done them well. Most of what we say and do is unnecessary anyway; subtract all that lot, and look at the time and contentment you'll gain. On each occasion, therefore, a man should ask himself, 'Do I really need to say or to do this?' In this way, he will remove not only unnecessary actions, but also the superfluous ideas that inspire needless acts."

Do few things and do them well, speak only when necessary: The wisdom behind the economy of action invoked here has not faded in its journey across the millennia. In fact, we are as likely to benefit from it as any of the generations that preceded us. Our narcissism and our worship of self-expression are relentless producers of unnecessary words. Our activism is irrepressible, and our quest for happiness is usually about adding things to do, not subtracting them. As devoted worshippers at the altar of consumption, we want more, and to have more we do more, only to realize eventually how wrongheaded our decision was. Marcus Aurelius's admonitions resonate with us by contrast. They remind us that more is not always better than less. In fact, less can give us more of what we really need—of what really matters.

THINKING IS HARD WORK

Delightful as it may be—thanks in part to the release of dopamine in our brain—thinking is also hard work. After we have engaged in it for a while, our levels of dopamine and glucose drop, and mental fatigue sets in. That thinking is tiring only begins to explain why so many people are wary of seriously engaging in it. Of course, some of us are naturally more inclined to think. Our formative years are a factor as well. If our family and friends did not model serious thinking for us, that was probably not without consequences. We may also avoid serious thinking because we do not want to get too closely acquainted with ourselves—just as many of us avoid looking at our faces in a mirror under an unforgiving light. By making us want to learn, humility keeps us willing to think. Unfortunately, in times like ours that condone and even encourage inflated self-opinion and reckless overconfidence, humility is in short supply. When we feel that we know it all, we are not inclined to spend a lot of time reflecting, let alone second-guessing ourselves. A further disincentive to think is the perception that the problems we are confronting are just too daunting. I may care about world hunger, but if I feel that nothing in my power can make a real difference, I may simply relegate this concern to a corner of my mind that I will seldom revisit. Finally, anti-intellectualism is still a force to be reckoned with. Americans admire full-time doers but are wary of full-time thinkers, especially when the results of the latter's thinking are not usable for practical purposes, such as finding a cure for cancer. The American ethos may not be easy to define, but one thing it is not is bookish. In fact, more often than in other parts of the world, in the United States "bookish" carries a connotation of "freakish." If asked if they would like their child to become an egghead, few parents would answer with an enthusiastic "Yes!" An intellectually gifted child will often be prevented from becoming a good thinker by the attitudes of his or her immediate environment and of society at large. Am I suggesting that we should retire from the world to live a life of contemplation? I am not. I am simply arguing that we should find the resolve to welcome deep thinking into our very active lives. The problem, then, becomes finding the time.

BUSY, VERY BUSY

A charming vignette graces the first page of William Powers's *Hamlet's BlackBerry*, one of the must-read books for those who want to understand our times. The vignette is about the author's friend Marie when she was a recent immigrant to the United States and still learning to speak English. Whenever he asked her how she was doing, she would respond, "Busy, very busy." The fact that her words never changed, and that she invariably uttered them with a big smile, gave Powers pause: "She seemed pleased, indeed ecstatic, to be reporting that she was so busy." It took him some time to figure out that Marie had been constantly hearing Americans say they were "busy, very busy"—to the point where she'd come to believe it was a polite formulaic response like "Very well, thank you." When was the last time you managed to sit down, sit still, and just think for a while? I mean losing yourself in the ebb and flow of serious reflection, neurons humming, and without letting your attention drift to the nearest computer screen. If you don't remember, you are certainly not alone. For many of us, serious thinking—the kind that makes a positive difference in our lives—has been shrinking like an endangered, pristine marshland threatened by suburban sprawl. The daily need to take action on short-term goals makes it difficult to reflect on the big picture at work. Much to the frustration of the best brains among us, work is increasingly for *doing,* not thinking. We are logging in a growing number of extra working hours that we scavenge in the rubble of what used to be leisure time. Thus, fatigue sets in at times of the day and the week when in the past our refreshed minds became hospitable to insight. Performance-addicted people do not think as much as they should because, engaged as they are in achieving, they look at thinking as a waste of time.

Maybe the family still feels like a sanctuary to chronically overworked Americans. The erosion of true leisure, however, has not spared the realm of the personal. Two-earner and one-parent households are forever pressed for time. Simple and ordinary tasks such as cooking, cleaning, and getting children ready for school can easily become burdensome chores to add to a daunting to-do list. "Overscheduled" is a recurring definition of today's family life, when fourth-graders need appointment calendars and unstructured child play is becoming a thing of the past. Very often it is as difficult to set aside some thinking time at home as it is at work. Good thinking requires time, and we believe we don't have it; it requires energy, and we are fatigued; it requires the conviction that it is good for us, and we have become indifferent to it; it requires concentration, and we have embraced entertainment. Ill at ease with the rare moments of true quiet still gracing our days, we fail to turn them into opportunities to assess who we are, where we have been, and what awaits us. It is more often the case that we hasten to disturb the unsettling void around us by turning to the closest digital screen. A dubious accomplishment of the often misguided age in which we live is its unparalleled perfecting of the art of distraction.

TIME WASTED

Gifted Canadian illustrator Melinda Stanley blogs both with words and with images (melindastanley.com/blog.html). In one of her long-gone entries, a stylish cartoonlike image of herself was sitting at a draftsman's table in an otherwise empty room, one of whose walls was covered from floor to ceiling with Internet logos: Facebook, Yahoo!, Blellow, Vimeo, cnn.com, Google, eBay, LinkedIn, Technorati, and so on. She was supporting her tired head with her left hand, and her face was a grimacing mask of comedic vexation. It only took a couple of seconds to realize that in her hour of exhaustion, her computer's screen had morphed into an elongated shape clearly identifiable as a shark with an enormous, toothed, wide-open mouth. The caption beneath the image read: "Sometimes I think about how big the internet really is and I feel as though it could swallow me whole." The Internet may not literally swallow us whole, but trillions of precious hours do disappear daily around the world as we sit transfixed at our remarkable digital machines. Melinda Stanley's cartoon can serve as a commentary on both the size of the Internet and our sizable Internet-related budgeting of time. Being in awe of the former should not prevent us from questioning the wisdom of the latter. One problem with our communication-saturated environment is that in it the actual value of what gets exchanged can become almost an afterthought. As the line separating the seriously consequential from the mostly entertaining keeps blurring, shallowness is entrenching itself as part of the human condition. Is it in the billions or trillions the numbers of workplace task interruptions that in any given day launch us into more or less furtive forays into the alluring realm of the digital? Do you really need to check the BBC headlines again, the silly video that is the viral craze of the moment, or the latest largely overlapping postings by half a dozen of your favorite news bloggers? Do you need to do it right *now*? What do those interruptions do to the quality of your work? The first, basic responsibility we have toward ourselves and others is choosing to think. In an age of distraction, that is also our challenge. Bypassing the ever-present temptation to divert and amuse ourselves is the first, crucial step toward an engaged and meaningful life. The next chapters will help you find the motivation and the time to do exactly that.

This is where you must decide whether you wish just to *read* this book or whether you wish to *live* it. Should you choose the latter, every chapter of this book ends with a number of exercises that are meant to maximize the benefits of the material covered in that chapter.

1. In the age of multitasking, is Marcus Aurelius's exhortation to keep things to a few inspirational or impractical?

2. Is finding time to think hard for you? What are the main obstacles you encounter? Is it family obligations, too much time spent at work, addiction to online amusement— to name a few? How can you overcome these obstacles?

3. Work on your motivation to think. Start making a list of the benefits that increasing your thinking time will bring you.

4. "Humility" is one of those words that seem to be covered by an archaeological patina. I do not remember the last time I heard a parent teach his or her child to be humble. It must have been decades ago. Besides the one mentioned earlier in this chapter, what are the uses of humility in today's world?

2

Finding the Time to Think

REDISCOVERING LEISURE

I have no time," we say, but we do, we always do. What we lack
is the will or wisdom to commit our time to goals that would be
smart of us to pursue. If you are really motivated to do something, you will *make* time for it. I am not arguing that you are
not busy. Most of us are. I am simply urging you to consider that
you are only as busy as you let yourself be. Leisure is waiting
around the corner. When we speak of "leisure" today, we seldom
speak of anything more serious than recreation or vacation. With
the words *skole* and *otium*, which we usually translate as "leisure,"
Greece and Rome in antiquity often designated a time being free
from the obligations of work that could be dedicated to the pursuit of knowledge and wisdom. No endeavors back then were
held in higher regard than those afforded by leisure. This view

implied that as humans we are at our best when, unencumbered with practical matters, we have the time and ease to think. We work in order to buy time free from work, proclaimed Aristotle, who considered *skole* (from which we derive our "school") humans' opportunity to fulfill their humanity and whose lofty idea of leisure influenced an entire civilization. Back in ancient Athens and Rome, access to thoughtful leisure was limited to a privileged few. At a time like ours when engaging in serious thinking could be possible for so many people, we are left to consider our widespread lack of willingness to do so. Since setting aside time to think is as important today as it was in Cicero's age, we need to rediscover the kind of leisure that is about exercising our minds. There is only one source of thinking time, and that is the time we spend doing something else. Once you have identified the things you usually do that you wish to cut to regain control of your time, go ahead without looking back. "Reduce," one of the environmental imperatives of our times, should be our constant concern. Imagine all of those things that make you impossibly busy as overbuilding. It is urgent that you restore ecological balance to your life by thinning out the sprawl of the trivial in it. We all need to find the resolve—to do fewer things and do them more effectively so that we can think more.

Learn to say no. Here is a subject missing in our schools' curricula. It is really too bad, because knowing how to articulate an effective and gracious refusal is a skill that we all could use in the most diverse circumstances of life. As a clear commitment to boundary setting, a firm "No" is a form of self-respect. It allows you to keep the time that belongs to you for the purpose of spending it at your discretion. When you feel guilty about saying no, repeat to yourself that your time is exactly that, *yours,* and you are not wronging anybody by exercising your privilege to employ it as you wish. If you have determined that "No" is your chosen reply, do not procrastinate in conveying it. You will be surprised how easy it is to say it once you have tried it. Also, the more you bring yourself to say no, the easier it becomes. A more effective way of finding time to think never existed. Warning: If your sense of self-worth is not as strong as it should be for your own good, chances are you will have to work on it before you get to the point of being able to assert yourself successfully.

Delegate. Giving other people work to complete on your behalf is never easy. Not many of us enjoy relinquishing control. Do it carefully, but do it. If you don't, finding time to think will become virtually impossible. Of course, if you have built a good team, your level of trust in your workers will be higher and consequently delegating will be easier.

Do things right the first time. Whether it's wallpapering your dining room or doing marketing research at work, take your time to do it right the first time. One reason we have no time to think is that we end up doing whatever we have been working on all over again. Yes, being diligent will be more time-consuming than being shoddy. But a shoddy job is not a complete job.

Be a conscientious manager. If you have managerial responsibilities, keep your unit staffed at optimal levels, strive for maximum fairness, do not skimp on communicating, and show a considerate disposition. Identifying and dealing with underperforming is part of your job and something you owe those of your employees who give their best. In general, do all you can to make working for you a positive experience. When you manage to do that, fewer workers will disengage, take sick days, or quit, which will allow your unit to function effectively. If all workers carry their weight, there will be more time for everybody to set aside for practicing the habits of attention, introspection, and reflection that you want to encourage.

Save time with the one-third solution. How many business lunches are you expected to attend in the next twelve months? How many do you *need* to attend? Look at your calendar for the *past* twelve months. How many business lunches did you attend? Thirty? What would have happened if you had not attended ten of them and had instead handled the business with a couple of telephone calls? Nothing dire, you guess? What if you decided to cut by one-third the number of lunches you are going to attend in the next twelve months? Again, probably nothing terrible would happen. It will just be a matter of deciding which of the meetings are going to be lunch and which telephone meetings. Now you have a finite number of lunches rather than an open one (which is good training in discipline). Think of them as tokens to spend carefully. There will be instances when your physical presence is going to be essential. Or you may choose to go for the simple reason that you like the company of the other person. Once your tokens are gone, however, you are out of luck, unless you borrow from the next twelve-month stash. All in all, if it looks as though you will save a considerable amount of time (and money) without jeopardizing business, do cut back. You can use the same system with all sorts of time-consuming activities.

Think for lunch and commute thoughtfully. Have you gotten into the habit of bringing a midday sandwich to your computer station? Does lunch mean updating your Web site, checking your e-mail, answering your phone, and firing off overdue messages on your BlackBerry while your food goes uneaten? The best gift you can give yourself is to leave your office every day at lunchtime and make sure you do not return before fifty minutes have elapsed. Take a walk, look for trees and a patch of grass, eat your salad on a bench—preferably a wooden one—and relax into thinking. Through practice you will get good at it. You will learn to enjoy thinking the way a wood-carver enjoys carving, a swimmer enjoys swimming, or a singer enjoys singing. Among the innumerable observations made by Sigmund Freud on the functioning of the human mind is that it derives pleasure from its own functioning.

You will look forward to this, your daily rendezvous with your own brain. Do you need to rethink the report you wrote for your boss? What can you do to increase the quality of teamwork in your unit? How can you help the foreign colleague who was hired only a week ago? Where are you now in your career?

Where do you see yourself five years from now? How do you see yourself within your organization? Is it still a good fit? Are you given the opportunity to contribute at your best? What space for growth do you have? What is the future of your industry? Your thinking does not have to be exclusively work related. Think about relationships, living ethically, and health and diet. The gamut of the issues to consider is up to you. However, do not crowd your daily agenda. Take your time to do justice to an issue before you move to the next. If you have time for only a couple of them in the allotted fifty minutes, so be it. Finally, consider that other underutilized thinking resource: commuting time. Make it a new year's resolution to turn your commuting time into thinking time. Give yourself a four-month goal: four months without radio, without your iPod, and without Internet surfing or texting while commuting. That way you can have a real sense of accomplishment in a relatively short amount of time.

Schedule your daily think time. Include fifteen uninterrupted minutes of pure thinking into every weekday. Focus not only on the practical needs of the moment, but also on big-picture issues. In fact, the more you are pressed by current concerns, the more important it is that you put some distance between you and them, if only for a brief amount of time. You may place your fifteen minutes at the beginning of your workday on Mondays, and you may sandwich them between appointments on Wednesdays. What matters is that you consider this daily appointment with yourself important enough to keep. Then, schedule an un-interrupted and undisturbed half hour of thinking on Satur-days and Sundays. When an opportunity to carve an extra thinking niche within your day presents itself, do not dismiss it by telling yourself that another will materialize soon enough. Take every thinking opportunity, even if the time at your dis-posal will allow you only one substantial thought. By doing so, without even realizing it you will do much more thinking than you would if you did not impose this discipline upon yourself.

Think with partners. Although there is no substitute for the thinking we do alone, do not forget dialogue. I am talking about a real dialogue, one that is productive because two persons bring to the table their knowledge and wisdom in a spirit of true cooperation. Dialogue is particularly useful in the first phase of a project when you do not know anything about it except for an idea, and at the end of it when you think you know everything. In the initial dialogue, you want to make sure that you don't fail to consider something crucial. In the end-of-project dialogue, you have a last opportunity to make an adjustment upon which the success of the project may depend. Good leaders schedule one-on-one meetings with their internal collaborators and their consul-tants at these times.

Turn "waiting time" into "thinking time." Nobody likes to wait. It bores us, it frustrates us, and it makes us anxious. Now, if waiting were just an occasional turnoff, it would not be worth serious attention, but waiting is a constant presence in our lives. No day goes by without our experiencing waiting time alienation. Waiting comes in many forms, but our feelings about it are fairly consistent. For most of us, it remains a waste of time and something to endure. That we have turned a natural part of the human condition into an unproductive stressor should give us pause. What if instead of resisting waiting, we made it our ally? What if we transformed it into a stress-free, stress-reducing, and fully lived time of personal choice? We need sanctuaries where we can seek shelter from the frenzy of contemporary life by slowing down to the pace of thinking. Reconceiving waiting can give us some of these sanctuaries. Granted, you may not find this a very easy shift, especially at first. Radical changes in mental disposition rarely click into place without effort. However, the rewards will make your effort worthwhile.

A few years ago, I simply decided that I would not let waiting bother me anymore. Once I made up my mind, taming waiting and making it dance to my tune was not difficult at all. A modicum of willpower did the trick. To this day, when I wait I seldom seek distraction. I do not want to kill time. I want to put on my thinking cap. Being able to put waiting to good use adds a remarkable amount of tranquillity to my days. I did it, so can you. Starting now, decide to stop dreading waiting. Whether you are looking at a two-hour wait before the ticket windows open for the concert you are going to attend or you are waiting for the traffic light to turn green, you can champ at the bit or relax and welcome the gift of precious time for your personal use.

NUTELLA NEWS

In 2009, the Radicati Group, Inc., a leading market research company in the field of technology, estimated that the number of e-mail messages sent worldwide on any given day during that year would total about 247 billion. The prediction was that the figure would climb to 507 billion by 2013. Now, we know that about 80 percent of such staggering output will be spam. But then there are the messages we send every day that are often only marginally more urgent than spam. And then there are our posts. Why do we do it? Easy: Mostly because we can. This was not a need before the technology existed. It is not that in the now almost archaeological past before social media we were saying to ourselves: "If there only were a way I could tell the whole world that I am switching from peanut butter to Nutella for breakfast!" The technology developed first, and then we developed the habit of using it trivially. We are enthralled by the ego boosting that can come from posting on the Net, so we jump from MySpace to Twitter, day after day digitally marking the territory of our identity. But if access to this technology disappeared overnight, would our lives be much poorer for it? I seriously doubt it, and I surmise that we would seek more offline connection. The time has come to question the wisdom of spending so much time online, where so much of what we do is technology-driven rather than real-need–driven. The smart thing to do is take some of that time to invest in serious, uninterrupted thinking. This need is becoming increasingly pressing in our desperately busy and stressful days.

1. Write a couple of pages about the benefits of rediscovering real leisure. Then draft your personal plan for returning leisure to your life.

2. For the next six weeks, keep a log of your scheduled sessions of uninterrupted solo thinking. Write your entry as soon as the thinking time you have set aside has expired, when your thoughts are still fresh in your memory. Record your salient thoughts and expand on them. Your entry can be just a list of the different thoughts you pursued, or you can write in a more structured way and more extensively. Your format and style can resemble what you would choose for a diary or a blog. You may find yourself returning to a topic from one session to the next and maybe the next as well. That's all right, too. By the way, science has determined beyond a doubt that writing about your life— present and past—can be good for both your body and your psyche. Among other things, it strengthens your immune system and reduces the damages of stress. So you don't have to stop writing after a few weeks. If that's what you want, keep writing—in good health.

Attention: Awareness and Much More

FAR MORE THAN YOU MAY REALIZE, YOUR EXPERIENCE, YOUR WORLD, AND EVEN YOUR SELF ARE THE CREATIONS OF WHAT YOU FOCUS ON. FROM DISTRESSING SIGHTS TO SOOTHING SOUNDS, PROTEAN THOUGHTS TO ROILING EMOTIONS, THE TARGETS OF YOUR ATTENTION ARE THE BUILDING BLOCKS OF YOUR LIFE.
—*Winifred Gallagher*

Everyone," William James wrote, "knows what attention is. It is the taking possession by the mind, in clear and vivid form, of one out of what seem several simultaneously possible objects or trains of thought. Focalization, concentration, of consciousness are of its essence. It implies withdrawal from some things in order to deal effectively with others, and is a condition which has a real opposite in the confused, dazed, scatterbrained state which in French is called *distraction*, and *Zerstreutheit* in German." The importance of attention was not ignored by antiquity, as we can glean, for example, from a page of Epictetus (55–135 CE), the Greek slave who became one of the great

P. M. Forni

Stoic thinkers: "There is no part of the activities of your life excepted, to which attention does not extend, is there? What, will you do it worse by attention, and better by inattention? And yet what other thing, of all that go to make up our life, is done better by those who are inattentive? Does the inattentive carpenter do his work more accurately? The inattentive helmsman steer more safely? And is there any other of the lesser functions of life which is done better by inattention? Do you not realize that when once you let your mind go wandering, it is no longer within your power to recall it, to bear upon seemliness, or self-respect, or moderation?" As an enabler of moderation, attention becomes in the words of Epictetus a handmaiden to wisdom. Rediscovering the importance of attention in our everyday lives is where our rediscovery of thinking must begin. This entails looking at attention in its discrete form, an attention that pauses on and takes in an object of interest before moving on to the next one. In other words, I mean the kind of attention that in our civilization appears to find itself in the throes of an unprecedented crisis.

BEDROCK OF THINKING

Comprising our faculties of awareness and focus, attention is the very bedrock of thinking. By constantly making us aware of our surroundings, it is crucial to our safety and well-being. Inattention causes eight out of ten traffic crashes in the United States—a powerful reminder of how high the attention stakes can be. When we are alert to our environment, we spot problems in their early stages before they become more difficult to manage. Not only does attention assess the world at lightning speed, it also works over lengthy periods of time, bringing us back to unfinished tasks. Attention is indispensable to the acquisition of learning and a necessity in scientific discovery. Thanks to the revolutionary technology of neuroimaging, today we know much more about how attention works than we did only a few years ago. In the process of studying the two neural networks that make awareness and focus possible, neuropsychologists such as Michael Posner discovered a third network that they called "executive attention." Interacting with other networks in the brain, executive attention is involved in—among other things—the controlling of emotions and the realization of goals. The book you hold in your hands was made possible by the work of the executive network.

Attention demands our respect as never before, not only because of its potential to better our lives, but also because of the challenge of living in an age of massive distraction. Ultimately, an information-rich world is a time-poor world, and a time-poor world is an attention-poor world. One reason we pay so little serious attention to the world around us is that there is too much to pay attention to. Not only do we consume information, information consumes us as well. A case in point is multitasking. A consequence of chronic time poverty, multitasking is our attempt to do the maximum amount of things in the shortest amount of time with the minimum amount of thinking. Thus, we spend a large part of our days in the mental state that Linda Stone—a distinguished expert on the impact of the new technology on our daily lives—calls "continuous partial attention." I doubt that from it we can expect intellectual breakthroughs. The good functioning of our attention skills depends on the good maintenance of our psychophysiological system. Do not skimp on sleep, maintain a balanced diet, keep yourself hydrated, and eat healthful snacks if you need an energy boost. Avoid stress whenever possible, and exercise regularly.

Attention's job can be as simple as registering an approaching fire engine's plaintive wail or as complex as the active, purposeful investment of mental energy in a challenging task. M. Scott Peck powerfully reminded us that through attention we give of ourselves for the sake of others. "The principal form that the work of love takes," he writes, "is attention. When we love another we give him or her our attention; we attend to that person's growth." Growth here can be more than a metaphor. You may remember the little children in the orphanages of Bulgaria and Russia who were in the news some years back. Because nobody ever held them, played with them, or cared for them, their growth was stunted. At such an early age, they were irreparably compromised in body and spirit. Their fate reminds us that attention is not only a cognitive faculty, but a moral imperative. Membership in the human club comes with the expectation that we will pay some degree of benevolent attention to other humans. What we tend to flourishes, what we neglect withers. In this respect, "attentive" is an interestingly hybrid word designating both someone who pays attention and someone who cares about the people he or she pays attention to. "Attentive" ends up closely resembling "thoughtful."

ALIENATED FROM THE PRESENT

I am sure you've seen many bumper stickers belonging to the "I'd rather . . ." genre: "I'd Rather Be Fishing," "I'd Rather Be Windsurfing," "I'd Rather Be Horseback Riding." The statements are straightforward, but when we stop to think about them, they reveal more than the preferred hobby of their car's owner. At issue here is having to live a less enjoyable moment (driving) while daydreaming of moments that are not (fishing, windsurfing, horseback riding). These bumper stickers tell the story of Western alienation. We have been chronically unable to be really present in the moment. Yet something is changing; in fact, a lot is. For increasing numbers of people, attention is a tool of choice for seeking relief from the turbulence and busyness of the world. By slowing down and paying attention to what lies in the folds of the moment, today's legions of the mindful receive peace of mind in reward. If life is valuable, it only makes sense to attend to it constantly. Focus on and do justice to whatever you are doing, no matter how mundane it may seem. If you are peeling an apple, peel it well. If you are preparing a presentation, do it attentively. Slay and bury the shifty dragon of the perfunctory. When working on a project, imagine yourself surrounded by a bubble that protects you from distraction.

Attention allows you to take full advantage of the innumerable opportunities you brush against in any given day. Because it demands a substantial investment of energy and time, it is certainly not an easy mental state to maintain. It is, however, when we are fully aware that we deal at our best with the world around us. The more aware you are, the more likely you are to notice, the more you reflect, and the more you are prepared to make the best decisions. The bottom line could not be clearer: Together with willpower, attention is the top building block of the fully engaged life. As such, it is the beginning of the good life.

KEEPING WORK AND LIFE TOGETHER

Is the prospect of yet another grueling week at the office casting a pall of dread upon your Sundays? If so, you have plenty of company. In the last several years, scores of opinion surveys have been telling us that large percentages of workers in the industrialized world associate work with misery. According to what seems like a million Web sites, the great problem of our times is how to achieve work/life balance. But to seek a balance between two things implies that they are different and separate. The more urgent problem is not how to balance work and life, but rather how to erase in our minds the line of demarcation that sets up the work/life dichotomy in the first place. Work is part of life, and it is precisely when we do not treat it as such that tension, disaffection, and alienation arise. As long as we neglect to claim work as part of life, as long as we *regard* it as a burden, it is going to *feel* like one. Every day, millions go to work predisposed to endure and leery to commit, which is just about the worst possible attitude to face work with. The first thing to do at work is to remain fully engaged in work. Focus and stay focused. Do not flee the present moment in search of something more appealing to the truant mind; that only makes you a hostage to your own distraction. Work with conviction and confidence in your abilities. When you make your mental horizon coincide with the task at hand; when you let yourself be absorbed into it to the extent that time stands still; when, in other words, you enter the state that Mihaly Csikszentmihalyi calls "flow"—the burden of work disappears. You are busily at peace. As you put them to use in the pursuit of a challenging and worthy endeavor, your focus, purpose, and resolve mysteriously generate contentment. Deeply gratified, you will most likely do all you can to keep experiencing this positive existential state day after day. Doing so will be a top factor contributing to the quality of your life. The bottom line: Concentrate at work; you will produce better results with less effort.

In sum, this is what attention does:

- It keeps you safe by alerting you to dangers.

- It allows you to concentrate on and decide what you are required to do in any given situation.

- It allows you to attune to people.

- It helps you achieve your goal when applied to a given task.

- It lets you focus on the present moment, allowing you to make the most of it.

- It increases your enjoyment of life.

- It helps make you a good listener.

- It makes other people feel validated.

- It produces insights.

- It makes you more productive.

- It enables you to collect information that you can use later in unexpected ways.

- It has healing powers.

DISTRACTION

Human attention has distraction built into its very operative mode. A minute or so into describing what your day was like, you clearly detect your spouse's interest wane. He nods absently, breaks eye contact, and casts a couple of wandering glances over your shoulder. You may be miffed, but humans are programmed to do exactly that. In prehistoric times, frequently interrupting whatever you were doing to scan your surroundings for fang-baring predators could make the difference between life and death. Those predators are no longer part of our lives, but a residue of our progenitors' lifesaving behavior is. Other reasons for our inability or unwillingness to focus include character traits such as self-absorption and low self-esteem, but also occasional conditions such as fatigue and sleep deprivation. The remarkable relationship between the mind and the world we call attention is one of the factors contributing to the quality of our lives that are under our control. It is too bad that so many of us are making use of it in a lackluster way. The good news is that although attention is not just a skill, it is certainly something that can be practiced. Thus, anybody's power of attention can be strengthened. Perhaps the next generations will have access to the formal attention training many of us regret not having received. In the meantime, methodically following the directions in the points at the end of this chapter will allow you to make giant strides. What remains of all our yesterdays if we spent them without attention and conviction? It is as though we never lived them—gone without a trace, never to return. What happened is clear: We did not value life enough to pay enough attention to it as it was happening. This is life, but not the good life.

Since it demands a substantial investment of energy and time, attention is not an easy state to maintain. However, it is when we are fully aware that we deal at our best with the world around us. The bottom line could not be clearer: The good life is a conscious life. The more you value life, the more you engage with it. The more you engage with it, the more you think your way through it. The more you think your way through it, the more effective you are as its trustee. It is then that you finally live out the elemental truth that in life there are no rehearsals and you only play for keeps. At a time when distraction is woven into the fabric of our lives, it is more urgent than ever that we make paying attention a planned and conscious effort. To look at the world with the eyes of an interested stranger for whom everything has the shine of the new is a rewarding way indeed of going through life. In every situation, for a few moments make sure you are *in* it but not *of* it—both actor and observer. Stop that extra moment to make sense of what the situation requires. Ask yourself, "What do I see?" "What does it mean?" "What can I do?" and "What are the interpersonal dynamics in this situation?" This process may sound time-consuming, but in reality it plays itself out in a matter of moments. Your answers to these simple questions will prepare you well to choose your course of action and face whatever life may bring you next.

1. Call it a diary, or call it your life log for your eyes only, one of the best attention exercises is to write about your days. A diary is an invaluable record of names, encounters, facts, impressions, and feelings. As you review in your mind everything worthy of note that happened during the day, you put it into perspective. You evaluate what you

did, you second-guess yourself, a detail comes to you that you thought you had forgotten, and so on. You are compelled to think. Your diary is a thinking tool. What about blogging instead, the way millions do around the world? A diary is different. It is not a dialogue with readers. It is something you want to keep to yourself and as such needs no filtering or polishing. You are completely free to go wherever the flying carpet of fancy takes you. Besides, knowing that later you will write about it, you will at times increase the attention you devote to what happens in your life at the very moment you experience it.

2. Disconnect the Internet for three hours each day and attend solely to the tasks at hand.

3. When you are engaging in conversation, make sure that you turn off your phone or any other wireless device and attend completely to what you're talking about.

4. Attention exercises do work and can be entertaining. Before going to sleep, try to remember what you heard on the news in the morning, the names of the characters and the plot of a novel you finished last week, and the items discussed in yesterday's meeting at work.

5. Through meditation you can detach yourself from toxic worries and obtain the relaxation, calm, and peace of mind that are otherwise so elusive today. A positive outcome of regular meditation is the sharpening of attention skills. Regular aerobic exercise has the same effect.

6. When it comes to paying attention to the world around you, are you coming up short because you are too focused on yourself? If so, explore the reasons behind that.

7. Reading what your children are reading allows you to show them how much content and detail they are expected to retain. Nancy Drew mysteries lend themselves to a conversation about the importance of attention, since attention is a core factor in the young sleuth's ability to solve her cases.

8. When it comes to the tree of the here and now, our ineptitude at picking its sweet fruit has been the rule. Strive to be present in the moment. Whether at school, at work, or at any kind of meeting or activity, concentrate, participate, and connect. Take notes, speak up, ask questions, and express opinions. Active participation is going to make you focus and help you remember what you are learning. Figure out how what you are learning is relevant to your interests and needs. Making these connections will help you keep paying attention.

4
Reflection: The Art of Going Over Your Life

THE CHOICE OF HERCULES

Once often quoted by moralists, "The Choice of Hercules," an
edifying Greek mythological story that Joseph Addison elo-
quently translated into English in the eighteenth century, is no
longer well-known. In fact, were it not for the surviving picto-
rial versions by old masters such as Annibale Carracci and for
Handel's oratorio, it would be virtually erased from our cul-
tural memory. According to the Greek historian Xenophon—
whose short text I paraphrase here—as he was coming of age,
Hercules felt compelled one day to sit down in a quiet place and
think about the life he wanted to live. The love-child of a mortal

mother and Zeus, he had already shown his mettle as an infant by strangling the two monster snakes sent by Hera, Zeus's wife, to destroy the offspring of her divine husband's tryst. By dint of brute force, he would soon complete the twelve labors thrust upon him by his father—thus gaining immortal fame. This day, however, was one not for the display of physical might, but rather for reflection and the exercise of willpower. So here he was, reflecting upon two opposite life paths—one of pleasure and the other of virtue.

As he was absorbed in thought, two women appeared, quite different in looks and demeanor. One was reserved and modestly attired, the other heavily made up and openly seductive. "Follow me," the latter said, "and you will be spared both the drudgery of work and the perils of war. No responsibility toward your fellow humans for you, Hercules, no cares, no sacrifices. Come let me show you a life of endless enjoyment of all of your senses." Hercules asked the lady her name. "My friends call me Happiness," she replied, "but my enemies call me Pleasure." Then the other lady—whose name was Virtue—stepped forward, eager to warn him not to fall for Pleasure's empty promises. "Whether it's the favor of the gods or the love of your friends that you want," she said, "whether it's honor from the state or the admiration of your fellow Greek, or perhaps abundant riches or might as a warrior, just remember that you will never acquire anything of consequence without effort." Scarcely had Lady Virtue completed her exhortation than Pleasure interrupted: "It is plain to see, young Hercules, how long and hard is the way by which this woman wants to lead you to her rewards.

Choose mine instead, which is short and easy." But in a scathing final rejoinder, Virtue reminded Hercules that a tragic pointlessness haunted the pursuit of pleasure for pleasure's sake. And that was just what Hercules needed to steel his resolve. The hard way—Virtue's way—was the right way. His decision was made. The story reminds us that reflection is the prelude to good decisions. Because we seldom set aside time to reflect, we are often unprepared for the important decisions upon which our future well-being depends.

THE MEANING OF REFLECTION

Reflection is the stuff of which decisions should be made. "Reflecting" is often used as a synonym for "thinking," but in fact it is not just any kind of thinking. When you reflect, you mull over and you ponder. It is thinking made serious by its content, intensity, and duration. It is often about revisiting past experiences to better understand them and use them to better cope with your current concerns. This is particularly important when those experiences are mistakes that would be painful and costly to repeat. After a relationship ends, uncompromising reflection can be crucial to not only your happiness, but that of your future partner. After a serious mistake at work, failing to reflect on its causes and consequences can cost you your job. You reflect to review the past, take stock of the present, and build a better future. The learning you acquire from reflecting on your experiences and those of others will depend on your willingness to ask yourself tough questions and to stick around for the uncomfortable answers. Here you must exercise caution. Do not dwell on the past unless you can learn from it. Do not look back to hurt yourself or others. The point is to use the past in ways that are beneficial to you.

Having tried in vain for quite some time to lose weight, you wish to find out the reason for your lack of success. Your first thought may be to shift blame: "My job is a sedentary one, and diets don't work." Reflection begins if and when you question those two improbable causes. Millions of people have sedentary jobs, but they also find the will and the time to exercise regularly. Is it true that diets don't work? Have you given the diets you tried a real chance? That you were not able to stay on a diet does not necessarily prove that the diet was bad. I am not saying that there are no bad diets. I am saying that more often than not, we are not good dieters. Looking back, you may realize that you start all your diets with a lot of motivation, following their instructions to the letter and quickly losing pounds. But at some point the weight loss slows, until eventually it stalls altogether, and before you know it, you are gaining weight again. What happened is that you were so emboldened by your initial success that little by little you relaxed your eating regimen. You blame the diet, return to your pre-diet eating habits, and eventually— many unhappy added pounds later—start the cycle again by trying another diet you will not give a chance to work. The clarity you gain through your reflection can be your point of departure from the failed attempts of the past. What you were doing was refusing to face responsibility for being unable to keep off your lost pounds. Your problem is keeping your motivation going after the first positive results. Starting another diet won't work until you work on yourself first. Why do you tend to overeat? Why is your motivation to curb your eating so shallow? Is your low sense of self-worth part of the problem? This is where you want to direct your thoughts now, and this is where reflection turns into introspection. In the next chapter, we will become better acquainted with this mode of thinking.

LEARNING FROM OTHERS' MISTAKES

Although learning from your own mistakes is certainly better than not learning at all, the problem is that damage is already done. You may have learned not to touch the hot pot, but you paid for that lesson with blistered fingers. That is why it is so important to learn from others' mistakes. "A smart man learns by his mistakes; a wise man learns by the mistakes of others," Confucius said. One could look at this almost ecologically. Since there are already so many mistakes to learn from, why contribute to the cluttering of the world by producing more? Do we really want to add to mistake pollution? Unfortunately, as Douglas Adams reminded us: "Human beings, who are almost unique in having the ability to learn from the experience of others, are also remarkable for their apparent disinclination to do so." Why? One reason is that learning from others' experiences requires more attention than learning from our own. It also requires empathy, that mixture of thinking and feeling that is ultimately moral imagination. To learn from the mistakes of others, you need to be motivated to focus on the other person's behavior, which will allow you to have a clear picture of what the mistake was and why it was one. You want to ask yourself to examine the cause or causes of the mistake. Was it fear, greed, envy, or maybe an insufficient sense of self-worth? Envision yourself in the situation. Would you be likely to make the same mistake? Why? Are there aspects of your character you need to work on? It is great that you found out now, so that you can prepare yourself. This is what the habit of reflecting allows you to do: prepare yourself to face the largest possible number of life situations with the best possible chances of success.

CONVERSING AND REFLECTING

We often approach our dialogues within a monologue frame of mind. We are so eager to tell our story, convey our opinion, or give our advice—whether it is being solicited or not—that we conveniently forget we are engaged in a give-and-take transaction. It is not just that we want to be heard, it is often the case that we want to make sure we control and dominate the verbal exchange. Thus, when the other person manages to get a couple of words in edgewise, we barely pay attention. Besides not being very civil, this is not very smart. It is not very smart because it prevents us from doing two very smart things: to validate others and to learn from them. More than anything, people want to be validated, and being listened to is one of the most gratifying forms of validation. Being a good listener is the hallmark of the real people person. Then, when you listen to what people tell you, you learn. Think of your verbal exchanges as conversational partnerships. Reflect upon what you hear. You will be doing justice to your partner's words and make your contribution more valuable. Valuable contributions will give you the reputation of a person whose opinions are worth listening to.

1. Do you enjoy engaging in reflection? Why? Why not?

2. What is the number one benefit of engaging in reflection? Why?

3. What does "The Choice of Hercules" mean to you?

4. Do you learn more often from your own mistakes or the mistakes of others? Do you have a sense of why?

5. What have you learned recently from your own mistakes?

6. What have you learned recently from others' mistakes?

Introspection: Self-Knowledge for Success

KNOW THYSELF

If you travel about a hundred miles northwest of Athens without straying from the coastal line of the Gulf of Corinth, you will find yourself at the feet of Mount Parnassus. On a southwestern cleft of that eight-thousand-foot limestone colossus known for being home to the Muses, the temple to Apollo awaits you at Delphi. It is here that the most famous oracle in all of Greece once spoke. Unfortunately, not much is left of the architectural marvel erected on a sacred place said to be the navel of the world. Yet just standing where once stood the vestibule to the temple may fill you with awe. This is where the words *Know thyself* were inscribed at the onset of the great Hellenic philosophical season. Not just a generic exhortation to pursue knowledge, the two-word humanist manifesto identified the self as the object of the intellectual quest. Introspection received at Delphi the most prestigious of endorsements.

"A reflective looking inward," "an examination of one's own

thoughts and feelings," is how *Merriam-Webster's Collegiate Dictionary,* 11th edition, defines "introspection," while *The Free Dictionary by Farlex* lists among its synonyms "self-examination," "reflection," and "soul-searching." When the object of your reflection is not the world *around* you but rather the world *inside* you, you have crossed into introspection territory. Ultimately, introspection is about getting to know oneself, a task that antiquity considered essential to the building of the good life. But why are we so seldom eager to take a good look inside us? Because it requires time and effort and because we are leery of what we might find. Part of introspection is asking difficult questions that may entail uncomfortable answers. Also, we have not been taught why we should engage in introspection and how. It is through introspection that we obtain the self-knowledge allowing us to bring positive change to our lives. By engaging in it, you will be able to see when it is not the world that needs to reform, but rather yourself. Do not waste that moment of clarity. You are the territory you need to discover before you set out to discover any other. If you are like most people, you are walking around with uncharted lands in your soul.

You can look inside you on your own, with a friend, or even with several other people under the supervision of an expert. You do not need any tools but can write down your thoughts in a journal if you wish. The important thing is that you actually do it. On a daily basis, carve some of your precious time to review the major choices you made in the past twenty-four hours, trying all the while to be as dispassionate as you can in your judgment of how you handled yourself. Every month or so, review the larger picture of your life. Your introspection may lead you to realize that you can't take care of your problems on your own. This is not a defeat. This is introspection serving you well. Be good to yourself and have the courage, the humility, and the good sense to seek help without delay.

SIGNATURE STRENGTHS

At the beginning of this century, pioneer of positive psychology Martin Seligman and his collaborators at the University of Pennsylvania embarked on an extensive comparative study of the world's religious and philosophical traditions. They were looking for a number of positive human character traits (what the Greeks and the Romans looked at as virtues) common to all of these traditions. After sifting through three thousand years of spiritual and ethical thinking, they eventually identified six virtually ubiquitous virtues. They were wisdom and knowledge, courage, love and humanity, justice, temperance, and spirituality and transcendence.

In his influential book *Authentic Happiness,* Seligman went on to list the routes—which he ends up calling "strengths"—that we can take to these virtues. Among them are love of learning, open-mindedness, social intelligence, bravery, perseverance, honesty, leadership, self-control, and prudence. All of us have "signature strengths," the strengths that we excel in, that we are excited about, that we are invigorated by, and that give us joy—in essence, the strengths that express who we are. It is by putting these strengths to work in everyday life that we obtain authentic happiness. Therefore we need to identify them and figure out the most effective ways to employ them. We also need to identify and focus on the strengths that do not come naturally to us, to improve our ability to work with them as well. Spending time in introspection, we build our identities and discover our values. Once we have given a good amount of thought to the important things in life, we have at our disposal a baseline for living. This means that when in everyday life we must decide how to act, we are not compelled to start from zero. Yes, in any situation of some consequence, it is important to think. But it is just as important *to have thought*. When we have structured our selves through serious introspection, our past helps us take care of both our present and our future.

ONE INTROSPECTIVE QUEST

Here is a possible and in fact not uncommon scenario of introspection. "Why do I find it so difficult to build good, long-lasting rapport? Is it me? I try hard, but when is hard too hard? Someone once told me that I am 'in-your-face friendly.' Maybe my eagerness to be liked feels unsettling and intrusive to others, so I end up turning off the very people I would love to establish a rapport with." This earnest self-examination might lead to the best thing to do in the circumstances: "I am going to relax and tone things down. To begin with, I am going to be more selective. I will invest my time and energy only when I see a real potential for a relationship based on shared values." This, however, is only the beginning in your journey of introspection. Ask yourself whether your eagerness to be liked is within the norm or not. If it is substantially above the norm, you want to know why that is the case. This is the time to account for that feeling of inadequacy that more than anything else seems to define who you are. Maybe as a child you were small for your age and struggled for several character-forming years to stand up for yourself. Maybe you have an older sibling you admire and whose charisma and accomplishments you always thought you could never match. Maybe your parents made you feel that pleasing them was the most important thing you could do and that you were not very good at it. Maybe it's other personal experiences. What's important is that you are starting to understand where the roots of your insecurity may be found.

Lack of self-esteem has been called the problem behind all problems. That may be an exaggeration, but rare indeed are the instances of self-inflicted misery that are not connected in one way or another to an insufficient appreciation of our personal worth. One of the ways low self-worth can hurt you is by predisposing you to fail. In fact, it often prevents you from even *trying* your hand at tasks that appear more daunting than they really are. Has underachieving become a way of life for you— both at work and in personal relationships? Do you not pursue the person you really like because he or she "is out of your league"? Do you settle for second or third best, and when you win him or her over, you lose because this is not what you really wanted? If so, your success is and will remain tainted. Sadly, you think that your real success would be to find the willpower to end the relationship. Many life-sustaining relationships are hurt—sometimes beyond repair—by complications arising from a poor self-image. The insecurity that makes us reluctant to assert ourselves can also make us diffident, defensive, and even hostile. A healthy self-image is arguably the most precious of our earthly possessions. This is something I know from personal experience. A sense of inadequacy has been an all-too-loyal companion of mine since my earliest years. Being aware of it, however, did not mean that I knew how massive its influence was in shaping my life or what I was supposed to do about it. Only in the last two decades or so did I come to fully realize that this deficiency complicated and eventually helped destroy my relationship with my father, made me the overachiever that I am, impelled me to leave my country and seek my fortune on another continent, and had quite a say in my choice of romantic attachments. In other words, it was a determinant of my destiny. It took me years and invaluable help from my wife, Virginia, to arrive at this point of clarity. There was comfort in just knowing the forces that shaped me and my life. And then I was ready for the next step: working on a more compassionate view of myself. It is work that will never end as long as I live but that has already been deeply rewarding.

THE CLOCK AND
THE WEATHER VANE

Are you happy with your sense of self-worth? Or, even more to the point, does your sense of self-worth allow you to be happy? Your answers will depend on whether you are a weather vane or a clock. A weather vane and a clock are both instruments meant to provide information, both depending on movement for their functioning. However, the source of their movement makes them essentially different. Whereas the weather vane's movement relies on an external force (the wind), the old-fashioned clock generates its motion thanks to an internal source (its wind-up mechanism).

All humans tend to function either more like weather vanes or more like clocks. Some people's life experience is largely driven by the external world. They see themselves the way others see them, and their moods are dictated primarily by external circumstances. Their mode of operating is reactive. The wind blows, the weather vane responds. They live outside-in. Their low levels of self-worth are often responsible for who they are. Then there are the people who habitually rely on an internal solid core of self-worth and firmly held convictions. They are the clocks. Our genes and the history of our personal experiences, and especially those of our formative years, are the building blocks of our character and contribute to making us either weather vanes or clocks.

ANOTHER INTROSPECTIVE QUEST

Perhaps you pride yourself on showing respect and appreciation for the values and customs of cultures around the world. In fact, not only do you not have a xenophobic bone in you—you are actually a veritable xenophile. The problem with your generous idealism is that it prevents you from considering that mores from one of the foreign cultures you champion are sometimes sharply at odds with those from another. One day, a friend points out to you that although your across-the-board acceptance may be high-minded, sometimes we are expected to choose—between right and wrong or even just better and worse. That's when you start to wonder: "Has my stance really been one of enlightened equanim-ity, or has it been a commitment to not committing? Is indis-criminate acceptance any better than prejudiced rejection? Have I been so ready to embrace all those customs because ultimately I did not care enough about what their ramifications mean for real people in real life?" Granted, it may take you some further think-ing to sort things out completely. For the time being, however, you managed to begin some serious work of introspection. By mustering the willpower to investigate an out-of-focus corner of your soul, you ended up growing in both self-knowledge and intellectual sophistication.

When engaging in introspection:

- You are not on trial. As a rule, you want to make intro-spection a journey of self-knowledge, not a fault finding expedition. However, the time may come when you discover that having wronged another, you need to make amends.

- You may not find what you are looking for. Keep looking. The more you look, the more you are likely to find. If you are comfortable with it, choose an introspection partner. Truth has been known to reveal itself within the give-and-take of dialogue.

- You may not like what you find. Take the lesson that is coming your way, but do not berate yourself. Consider it a success that you were able to look at yourself honestly and recognize a fault as easily as you might recognize a strength. Now that you have brought the problem to the surface, you are in a position to do something about it. Although you may not like the part of you that you have discovered, you can take comfort in the fact that there is another part of you that allowed you to make the discovery.

- You need the resolve to change what you do not like in yourself.

- Moderation is key here, as it is in so many aspects of a life well lived. A constant gauging of your emotional state is more of an obsessive practice than introspective. If you see yourself going in that direction, you know it is time to find a way to keep under control your obsessive impulses. Life is meant to be lived, not to be relentlessly monitored and analyzed.

1. To get a clearer picture of your identity, ask yourself the following questions:

   Are you shy? Are you extroverted, gregarious, or neurotic? What do you think contributed to making you who you are? Commit to two scheduled introspective sessions per week. Record the main issues you tackle.

2. Use the following questions in your introspective tasks:

   Am I a good person? Am I *being* a good person? Why should I be one? What gives meaning to my life? Do I have a healthy sense of self-worth? Why is it not as strong as it could be? What don't I like about myself? What am I going to do about it? What are my strengths and weaknesses? How can I capitalize on the former and keep the latter from hurting me? What do I really care about? Am I a taker or a giver? At what point in my life am I? Where do I go from here? Should I change? Am I just the wronged party, or am I part of the problem as well? What do I owe my fellow human beings? How can I make a positive difference in the lives of those around me? Why didn't I admit that I was wrong? What would have happened if I did? Did I wrong someone today? Did I show empathy when it was required? Do I need to set aside more time to keep asking and answering questions like these?

3. Every Friday afternoon, choose one of the most difficult decisions you had to make during that week and examine it. Ask yourself: "Did I make the right decision? How

could I have made a better decision? How did the decision relate to my sense of self?"

4. While writing this book, I asked my undergraduate students a number of questions about their thinking habits. The first was, "When is the last time you sat down alone with the sole purpose of introspection or reflection?" This is—almost untouched by editing—Claire's response:

Yesterday is the last time I sat down with the sole purpose of introspection—though perhaps this answer is not entirely true. I try to write every day, if only for a few minutes, and I usually begin this practice (warms my mind up) by recording certain phrases, images, linguistic sounds, what have you, that have recently resonated with me. This invariably leads to a period of stillness, during which I'm simply thinking about what things mean, or how to respond to an action, or why something has resonated with me so strongly. I also find that when I am reading, which I also try to do every day, I often pause to think about language or character, or more often even, how the poem or story appeals to me on a personal level and how I relate to it. This thinking often transitions into other avenues of tangential thoughts which lead off into seemingly unrelated ideas. I wish I could be a speed reader sometimes, and I often wish I could focus on the task at hand and not be distracted by ideas that blossom from the primary task. Maybe someday I will be this way, but I doubt it. In any case, to answer the question I don't necessarily sit down with the intention of having deep thoughts (though it

*suddenly occurs to me that I do take walks with this intention)
but it invariably occurs when I read or write.*

Claire's response deserves attention on more than one level.
There is her dedication to reading and writing; there is her
minute attention to the thinking processes (after all, she did
not *have* to be analytical; mine was a "when" question, not a
"why" or "what" one); there is her crystal-clear awareness that
thinking originates both in reading and in writing; and finally there is the sense of the pleasure she derives from losing
and finding herself in all three cognitive domains. It is my fer-
vent hope that there are many Claires out there quietly making the world a better place by just being good thinkers. Now
it's your turn to write about the last time you sat down alone
to engage in introspection or reflection.

6

Exercising Self-Control

A LITTLE SELF-MASTERY CAN IMPROVE THE QUALITY OF YOUR LIFE AS WELL AS THE QUANTITY. IF YOU ARE A MAN, IT CAN PRESERVE YOUR MARRIAGE, SINCE A STRONG PREDICTOR OF MARITAL STABILITY IS THE HUSBAND'S ABILITY TO CONTROL HIS IMPULSES. AND IF YOU'RE A STUDENT, IT CAN LEAD TO HIGHER LIFELONG EARNINGS, SINCE YOU ARE LIKELY TO DO BETTER—AND GO FURTHER—IN SCHOOL. STUDIES OF TEENAGERS HAVE FOUND THAT SELF-DISCIPLINE IS A MUCH BETTER PREDICTOR OF ACADEMIC PERFORMANCE THAN IQ—AND MAY ACCOUNT FOR THE SUPERIOR GRADES OF GIRLS, WHO DISPLAY MORE OF IT. SELF-CONTROL IS ASSOCIATED WITH MORE EDUCATION, LESS VIOLENCE, LOWER ALCOHOL AND DRUG ABUSE, HIGHER EARNINGS, AND AN OPTIMISTIC OUTLOOK—BUT ONLY MODERATE OPTIMISM.

—Daniel Akst

NOTHING IN EXCESS

In one of the most poignant fables of antiquity, Daedalus is a skillful Athenian craftsman with a troubling past. Unable to bear the thought that the talent of his nephew Perdix might one day obscure his own, he pushed him off a cliff of the Acropolis. That the merciful gods transformed the falling Perdix into the bird that still bears his name—the partridge—did not make Daedalus's action any less murderous. While living as an exile on the island of Crete, Daedalus has a new opportunity to put his craft to work. At King Minos's behest, he builds a labyrinth as the prison house for the Minotaur, the monster born to Pasiphaë, the king's wife. Determined that Crete's population remain unaware of the labyrinth and the story behind it, Minos has no compunction in imprisoning also Daedalus and his son Icarus. Crafty Daedalus soon plans the most daring of escapes: Father and son will fly to freedom. After assembling makeshift wings, he straps them to his son's body and his own, instructing Icarus not to fly too close to the sun, lest its heat melt the wax that keeps the wings together, or too close to the ocean, lest they become waterlogged. He will have to be very careful and keep a steady middle course.

As they ascend together, the father is still instructing the son. The wisdom of ripe age, however, is often powerless over the foolishness of youth. The elated youngster soon forgets all warnings as he flies ever closer to the sun and out of his father's sight. It is soon in vain that he desperately flaps his arms, since the wax of his wings has already melted in the heat, just as in vain he invokes his father's name as he plunges into the sea. Daedalus in distress calls out for Icarus as well, but when he sees the feathers scattered upon the surface of the water, he understands what happened, and the only thing he can do is curse his own talent as a craftsman.

Greek thinkers of antiquity saw the good person as someone able to choose rationally and therefore moderately among the options of moral consequence that life presents us with all the time. "Know thyself" was not the only inscription in the temple of Apollo in Delphi. Another one, "Nothing in excess," graced its front. Temperance was for Plato a major virtue. Aristotle conceived of virtue as a repudiation of extremes. Courage, for instance, occupied a median space between cowardice and foolhardiness. This middle way the Greeks called *mesotes*, but they also coined the word *sophrosyne*, which, while still carrying the meaning of moderation, pointed to an excellence of a higher order. The much-admired person who embodied it, the *sophron*, was an accomplished student of human nature and the natural world—all of which served him well in decision making, an essential factor in the successful pursuit of the good life. That a word meaning moderation also meant wisdom is a clear indication of the high esteem in which the Greeks held the ability to control the passions. Icarus, who fails to steer a steady middle course between the ocean and the sun, symbolizes all mortals failing to take the virtuous middle way in the vicissitudes of life. He is an archetypal anti-*sophron*. By the way, far from being an exclusively Greek phenomenon, the moral stance of eschewing extremes is widely present in human cultures. For instance, it is central to the teachings of the Buddha, who saw wisdom's way as a path to liberation through moderation.

JUST DO IT?

In the summer of 1988, Dan Wieden, a Portland advertising executive retained by Nike, was looking for a theme that would bring together the different elements of the campaign he was working on. For some reason, the last words uttered by convicted killer and Norman Mailer protégé Gary Gilmore as he was facing the firing squad came to his mind. Nobody at the time could foresee that the stark, short phrase he came up with by modifying Gilmore's words only slightly would make advertisement history. "Just Do It" went on to become one of the most memorable, admired, and effective advertising slogans of all time. It was selected by *Advertising Age* as one of the top five slogans of the twentieth century, it was inducted into the Advertising Slogan Hall of Fame, and its campaign is featured in the Smithsonian Institution. What are we to make of these three words that became such a catchphrase for an era? The flattering interpretation of Nike's slogan is that it prods procrastinators to do things—such as exercising—they know are good for them. However, it is almost impossible not to perceive in it an invitation to act without thinking. Sheer elementary prudence suggests that we collect facts and consider consequences before we act. To behave ethically, we need to slow down, notice others, feel empathy, and evaluate our options. Both prudent and ethical actions depend on time. "Just do it" evokes a temporally flat, amoral universe. Nike gave its young clients license to follow their impulses.

At the 2008 Summer Olympic Games, the prodigious athletic exploits at the Beijing Water Cube of a twenty-three-year-old from Baltimore, Maryland, became the event's hottest ticket. The whole world watched with trepidation and cheered as Michael Phelps, with boy-next-door looks and a superhuman lung capacity, swam his heart out to capture a record eight gold medals. With a total of fourteen career gold medals, Phelps left Beijing as the most decorated Olympian in the history of the modern Games. He was being hailed by many as the greatest athlete of all time. He had adoring fans in the millions and tens of millions of dollars in product endorsement contracts. In the summer of 2008, Michael Phelps was the toast of the world. Then, six weeks after his glory laps in Beijing, he was photographed at a party in Columbia, South Carolina, smoking a marijuana pipe. About three months later, having found their way to the pages of a London tabloid, the incriminating pictures stirred dismay around the world. Phelps (halfheartedly) acknowledged his mistake, but the damage was done. The bulk of the media coverage focused not on the gravity of the transgression, but rather on the mindlessness that made it possible. "What was he thinking?" was the question that implicitly or explicitly kept surfacing in news story after news story. Of course, it was more an expression of incredulity than a real question. The most likely answer, however, is very simple: He was not. I doubt that Michael Phelps sat down and said to himself: "Here I am. I can go ahead and use this pipe, break the law, maybe lose my reputation, and end up with half the world on my case, risking the loss of millions in sponsorship contracts in the process. Do I really want to do this?" My guess is that the twenty-three-year-old on top of the world did not stop to think. He acted out the Nike slogan. He just did

On the positive side, virtues seem once again to be in the ascendant. Restraint may acquire—albeit under a different name—an increasingly higher profile thanks to the environmentalist concern about wasting resources and our reduced affluence. Neo-hedonism notwithstanding, it remains self-evident that no society could survive if its members did not choose—frequently and predictably—restraint over impulse. It is also self-evident that refraining from intemperate action is a primary factor in the quest for a happy life. By now we are all familiar with the notion of the world as a global village. But for many of us it took the current crisis originating in the American financial markets to give a clearer sense of the global interconnectedness and interdependence of our lives. The devastating losses on Wall Street triggered similar losses in Asia, Europe, and Australia. Soon, the pall of gloom cast over the lives of Americans was affecting billions around the world. Among the many points for reflection we can find in the world crisis of 2008, a major one is that since we are interconnected, no action of ours is without consequences for other people. And since our actions have consequences for other people—intended and unintended—we must accept that there are limits to our freedom to act. It is when we go about our everyday lives with a constant awareness of these two basic features of the human condition that we behave as ethical agents. Some limits are prescribed by the law, others are not but are important as well. Both kinds require restraint, the willingness and ability to curb our needs and desires for the sake of effective relating and connecting at our best with other people. But restraint is also at the core of a responsible

HELPING YOURSELF
BY HELPING OTHERS

As I write these words, a book called *Blink* is marking its 134th week on the *New York Times* bestseller list. The continuing social phenomenon–sized success of a three-hundred-page argument for the soundness of snap decisions offers the opportunity for a couple of observations. While we were not looking, we entered a world in which impulsiveness had a positive connotation and a high profile. This can give the wrong and pernicious impression— especially to the younger generations—that self-control and prudence are hindrances rather than assets. On the contrary, they have not stopped being crucial to the quest for the good life. The best way to rediscover self-control is to rediscover Immanuel Kant's principle of respect for persons and make it part of our way of being in the world. A foundation of moral thinking, the principle states that we ought to look at others as ends in themselves rather than merely as means for reaching our goals and fulfilling our desires. This implies that we all have equal dignity as persons and that to disregard others' happiness as we pursue our own is reckless and wrong. This is where self-control comes in. Exercising self-control does not mean refraining from seeking our own advantage; rather, it involves refraining from doing so at another's expense. Life doesn't have to be a zero-sum game. If you help others to reach their goals, disinterestedly and whenever you can, you will be surprised by the handsome rewards awaiting you. Reaching your own goals by helping others reach theirs is self-control at its best. It is often the case that indirect rather than direct pursuit ends up bringing success in life. Indeed, this is true for the pursuit of happiness. We usually obtain happiness not because we have been very good at pursuing it directly, but because we have been good at doing something else—namely, at building a good life day after day. Happiness is not a destination, it is a daily by-product of a life well lived—and self-control is a cornerstone of such a life. Although it may limit the amount of fun you can have in your life, self-restraint is not a threat to happiness. In fact, happiness could not exist without it.

THE POWER OF SELF-REGULATION

The Framers of the Constitution assumed that the majority of their fellow citizens would respect just authority and that their pursuit of personal interest would be bound by concern for the common good. On October 11, 1798, John Adams addressed a memorable letter to the officers of the Militia of Massachusetts. Concerned about the viability of the experiment that was America, in the space of a few lines Adams twice identifies the sole conditions under which—vulnerable and fragile as they are— governments can survive and prosper: "We have no government . . . capable of contending with human passions unbridled by morality and religion. Avarice, ambition, revenge or gallantry, would break the strongest cords of our Constitution as a whale goes through a net. Our Constitution was made only for a moral and religious people. It is wholly inadequate to the government of any other." Keeping appetites in check, then, is a condition for the survival of both order and freedom. No effort to impose lawful regulation upon members of society can succeed in the absence of self-regulation.

OBEDIENCE TO THE UNENFORCEABLE

It was with insightful clarity that in 1924 John Fletcher Moulton, a British judge and mathematician, laid out what he called "the three great domains of human action." First there are things we do because the laws of the land compel us to. Lord Moulton called this the domain of positive law. Then there are others we do with unrestricted freedom, which Moulton called the domain of free choice. Positive law and free choice do cover a wide range of human actions. But between these two domains, Moulton saw a third, and vast, one. He called this the domain of obedience to the unenforceable, and thought it was of paramount importance in the lives of societies. Voluntarily stopping by the wayside to give the police your statement as a witness to a car accident is an example of this category of behaviors. "The real greatness of a nation," Lord Moulton observed, "its true civilization, is measured by the extent of this land of Obedience to the Unenforceable. It measures the extent to which the nation trusts its citizens, and its existence and area testify to the way they behave in response to that trust." The more a society relies on this domain of self-regulation, the less need it has to legislate, and the less it will be plagued by coercion, conflict, and litigation.

HOW TO STRENGTHEN
SELF-CONTROL

The good news is that you have a degree of control over your self-control—namely, you can make it stronger by following a set of simple recommendations.

• Remember the "Don't flirt, don't fall" rule. Do all you can, that is, not to seek out the sources of your temptation, whatever they may be. If you love chocolate but can't eat just a small amount, don't keep it around. Self-control begins with freeing your environment from the threats to your self-control.

• Strengthen your fortitude by testing it. Earmark every day of the week for something that is at the same time good for you and not appealing. For instance: Make Mondays no-snacking-between-meals days; Tuesdays, try turning your commute into an introspection session rather than listening to talk radio or surfing the Net; and on Wednesdays, take care of things that have been languishing for weeks in procrastination limbo. And so on.

• Work on your resolve. You may both enjoy and profit from taking the time to write down your grand plan (for instance: junior year abroad, senior year internship at the U.S. Senate, two years with Teach for America after graduation, law school, clerkship with a judge, law firm job). A written resolution is often more binding than a nonwritten one.

• Strengthen your body and you'll strengthen your powers of self-control. Healthful nutrition, regular sleeping hours, a sane mixture of engagement in work and the pursuit of meaningful leisure, intellectual stimulation and physical exercise, tolerable levels of stress, good social support, and a realistic sense of self-worth all contribute to your well-being and in turn contribute to your ability to control yourself.

And then there is patience. One of the reasons we are not as proficient in self-control as we could be is that we are not trained in being patient. Patience may not be glamorous, but it is a virtue and a skill we rely on almost as often as we do on self-control. In fact, patience is a form of self-control. You are patient when you stop resenting reality for not conforming to your desires, which is to say when your mind is set to accept what you can't change. Whether it's waiting in line at the supermarket's checkout counter, coping with the consequences of a canceled flight, seeing your contribution at work go unrecognized, or enduring painful physical therapy after being injured in a serious traffic accident, patience is there to help you if you find it in yourself to embrace the present moment rather than pushing it away. Patience is the ability to relax, having realized and truly internalized that disruption, disappointment, nuisance, uncertainty, sickness, hardship, and adversity are not tears in the fabric of reality, but the fabric itself. Learn to expect them and you are halfway to accepting them. Learn to accept them and the quality of your life will improve exponentially. All this should not make you forget that patience is also the humble handmaiden of hope. Part of her job is to keep alive in you the prospect of a better future. It is patience that allows you to endure hardship without despair by reminding you that "this too shall pass." One final word of warning: Don't mistake inertia for patience. The former is a form of weakness, is passive, and lets you accept what you should not. The latter is a form of strength; it is active and enables you to accept what you should.

SELF-RESTRAINT AND SELF-EXPRESSION

Once upon a time, self-expression was only as good as what you could express and how you would go about expressing it. Self-restraint, by contrast, was an intrinsically good thing, not in conflict with self-expression, but rather a necessary provider of discipline and form. Today's ego-worshipping global tribe extols self-expression or—more precisely—the idea of self-expression as an intrinsically good thing. Coincidentally, the perception is pervasive that self-restraint is the enemy of self-expression, the inhibitor of the spontaneity that is supposed to be one and the same with our creative drive. One of the most unfortunate, and indeed sophomoric, developments in our culture is to have set up self-expression and self-restraint as opposites, with the latter as the black-hatted bad guy. Afraid that if they openly disapprove of their children's behavior they will inhibit their self-expression, today's parents are much less inclined to parent than parents in the past. One dire consequence of this leniency is legions of self-absorbed youngsters inhabiting a de facto no-fault zone of their mind and therefore not in the best position to admit to their mistakes. This means that they are not equipped with the unsparing clarity needed to learn from them. Learning to reflect is of special importance to these youngsters as they become adults if they are to undo at least part of the damage caused by no-fault child rearing.

BENJAMIN FRANKLIN'S STYLE OF RESTRAINT

In his utterly charming and wise autobiography, Benjamin Franklin reminds us what a bright early star in the firmament of self-improvement literature he was. He records his foolish delight as a young man in showing off as a spinner of artful arguments. For years, he ensnared his opponents with rhetoric—not to say sophistry—"entangling them," he admits candidly, "in Difficulties out of which they could not extricate themselves, and so obtaining victories that neither myself nor my Cause always deserved."

The smart and ambitious young Franklin eventually understood that his take-no-prisoners strategy was not endearing him to the world and that his somewhat arrogant way of besting his opponents had been self-defeating. His life-changing intuition was in essence the same one upon which Dale Carnegie at a much later time would build his masterful manual, *How to Win Friends & Influence People*—namely, that our ticket to success in life is the ability to make others feel good about themselves. So as he approached full maturity, Benjamin Franklin radically changed the way he spoke. He dropped all expressions of bold self-assurance, such as the "certainly" and "undoubtedly" that had appeared so frequently in his speech, replacing them with markers of personal opinion such as "It appears to me, or I should think it so *or* so for such & such Reasons, *or* I imagine *it to be so, or* it is so if I am not mistaken." "This Habit," he writes, "I believe has been of great Advantage to me, when I have had occasion to inculcate my Opinions & persuade Men into Measures I have been from time to time engag'd in promoting." He understood very well that this gentler way was effective in preventing or softening resistance on the part of those he wanted to convince. He reinvented himself as a smart, restrained communicator, and his move was crucial in securing the long decades of success that lay ahead.

LUCIA: A PORTRAIT IN GRACIOUS SELF-CONTROL

If asked what makes a person a "people person," most of us would probably come up with adjectives such as "self-confident," "outgoing," "friendly," and "gregarious." Maybe some of us would picture the exuberant friend who becomes a little boisterous in his or her role as the life of the party. Not many of us, however, would immediately single out "restrained," "tactful," or even "considerate" as typical character traits of a people person. But these are the traits I associate with my friend Lucia, and to me she is a wonderful example of a people person. A couple of days ago, when I happened on a statement by Maya Angelou, my thoughts drifted to Lucia. "I've learned," said Dr. Angelou, "that people will forget what you said, people will forget what you did, but people will never forget how you made them feel."

It is not that Lucia consciously tries to validate people, but in her presence people can't help feeling that she is naturally appreciative of the good she perceives in them. All it takes is her sincere smile accompanied by a few notes of the warm and captivating Venetian intonation of her speech. Lucia's life has not been an easy one. She lost her husband when her two children were twelve and ten, and she raised them as a single mother. I do not know how much of her character was forged by adversity. What I can tell is that there is no bitterness in her and that Marco and Leonardo have grown into remarkably bright and thoroughly decent young men. They may be independent and successful, but they are also unafraid of showing that they adore their mother.

Blessedly provided with a healthy sense of self-worth, Lucia does not feel that she must prove herself to the world all the time. Although she thrives on seeking agreement and getting along, this does not prevent her from coming to a fiery defense of her most valued principles. She is comfortable with her own silence and stillness, which contributes to making her a good listener. The fact that she is reserved yet cordial draws people out. In essence, she is an accomplished—although unassuming—connector and communicator. If, as the dictionary says, *affable* indeed means "gentle and gracious," Lucia is a portrait in affability. When I asked Lucia what made her happy, without hesitation she pointed to her satisfaction in what she has achieved as a parent. Then she mentioned the widening of her horizons through travel and meeting new people. Finally, she revealed that what makes her happy is ultimately making others happy.

FUN AND HAPPINESS

As I was thinking about Nike's slogan "Just Do It," I came across another unredeemably ill-conceived pronouncement from a high-profile American company. "If it's not fun, why do it?" has been Ben & Jerry's corporate motto ever since hippie ice-cream guru Jerry Greenfield first asked this question at a company retreat in 1979. Sorry, Ben & Jerry's, but there are millions of things that we want or need to do in this world even if they are not fun, from paying our bills to undergoing dialysis, from giving our seat on a bus to a pregnant woman to apologizing to a friend, from going to work on a rainy Monday to firing a dedicated employee. The staggering amount of misery we bring upon ourselves in life depends to a large extent on our clumsy conflating in our minds of fun and happiness. Fun is what you get from an amusement park ride, happiness is what you get from a life well lived. Fun is eminently transitory, happiness can last an entire season of life—or an entire life, for that matter. Fun comes with the awareness of having it, but it is often only by looking back at our past that we discover we were happy. I have said many a time that if our schools succeeded in teaching the difference between fun and happiness, with just that accomplishment they would justify their existence. It is an exaggeration, but one I am always tempted to use to make a point. And the point is that although there is certainly a place for fun in our lives, the unthinking or unrestrained embracing of fun can—and often does—hinder the pursuit of happiness.

1. "Nothing in excess" is part of our philosophical and spiritual legacy. What are some of the things that you tend to do in excess and that you would be wise to keep under more effective control?

2. Just like Benjamin Franklin, you may reach a point in your life when you feel the need to overhaul your communication style. Do you, like him, need to exercise more restraint in the manner in which you speak? What could you do to improve your skills in this area?

3. Is your problem the opposite of Franklin's? Maybe your reserve and deference to your co-workers are working against you, making your overall demeanor too close to self-effacement. Are you in urgent need of lessons in assertiveness, taking the initiative, and showing everybody that you believe in yourself? Ask a couple of close friends and trusted colleagues how you come across, and when you have a clear picture, plan the necessary changes.

4. What are the consequences for individuals and societies when their members choose feeling good over being good?

5. How can one argue that self-restraint is not the natural enemy of self-expression?

7

Embracing the Positive

WE ARE WHAT WE THINK. ALL THAT WE ARE ARISES WITH OUR
THOUGHTS. WITH OUR THOUGHTS WE MAKE THE WORLD.
                                —*Siddhartha Gautama (Buddha)*

WHAT IT MEANS TO BE POSITIVE

It is seven o'clock in the morning and you wonder if your day is
going to be hard and unremarkable again. As you pull your car
keys out of your pocket or purse, it occurs to you that these
days are your life and they will not come back. You begin to see
that this is the only life you have in which to experience fun,
joy, contentment, and happiness. And then, when your spouse
wishes you good luck on your meeting, your newly found clarity tells you that most of what goes into making a meeting or a
day go well is dependent not on luck at all, but rather the result
of your own doing. Your day will not have a chance to become
successful without the input of your attitude and skills. The
thoughts we carry around in our heads make us the people we
are and give shape to the lives we live. To use James Allen's

metaphor, our thoughts crystallize into habits and our habits solidify into circumstances. Circumstances, then, will be good or bad depending on the thoughts and habits from which they derive. Nurture kind thoughts and you will be kind; generous thoughts and you will be generous; positive thoughts and adversity will not seem so daunting.

I am not arguing that reality exists only as a mind construct. We *are,* however, all under the spell of an illusion of sorts. The illusion is that we are one with life, when instead life's experience is always a mind-mediated one. As the great Stoic philosopher Epictetus observed with utter clarity two thousand years ago, it is not things in themselves that disturb us, but rather what we think of them. Mondays are not intrinsically evil aberrations devised by sinister gods seeking entertainment in our misery. Mondays are only as bad as you make them according to the attitude with which you look at them. Similarly, a weekend at the beach is only as good as the attitude you pack with your flip-flops. It is not that you need to turn your life upside down. To paraphrase Henry David Thoreau, you just want to affect the quality of your day. To relate to your day at your best, look at it with *interest* rather than *judgment.* Do not be rigid, thinking that in order to be good it must conform to fixed criteria. If you do, disappointment and disaffection are inevitable. Asking not *whether* your day is going to be good, but rather *in what ways* it is going to be good is Positivity 101.

For some people, positive thinking comes naturally, but many others have to work at it. You may function positively in certain circumstances and not in others. Of course, the more difficult the circumstances, the more accomplished a positive thinker you need to be to keep thinking positively. Positivity comprises gratitude for the past, acceptance of the present, and anticipation of a fulfilling future. It comes with a reasonable amount of self-appreciation and a feeling that one's goals in life are meaningful. Positivity enables you to expect the best and also make the best of what situations allow. Those with a positive outlook laugh and smile a lot. They tend to see defeats as momentary rather than permanent and caused by external circumstances rather than personal error. Positivity gives toxic worry a wide berth, and by limiting the overall impact of stress, it promotes health and well-being.

Being a positive thinker does not mean going through life in a Pollyanna-ish state of mind, unwilling to face its harsh realities. Positive thinking is about acceptance rather than denial. If you wake up anxious one morning, you accept the fact and then put it in perspective. The positivity is in your acceptance and in what you do even with a negative. For example, you might tell yourself that your anxiety is likely to point to a long-standing problem. Your psyche may have resorted to giving you anxiety because you kept ignoring the problem instead of solving it. Now you have made anxiety your ally. This has the effect of making you do something more constructive than complaining—namely, try engaging in introspection to find out what the problem is and how to solve it.

MAKING PROBLEMS
WORK FOR YOU

Real positive thinking is smart thinking. Take work, for example. There are plenty of reasons to dislike it. It curtails freedom, it requires untold expenditures of energy, and it is repetitive, among other negatives. Coworkers are no walk in the park, either. One-third of American workers identify the people at their workplace as the number-one cause of stress at work. If you are inclined to think about work along these lines, a few positive affirmations will not bring about the sea change you are looking for. A real insight might. How we think about work determines how we feel about it. No matter what you do, work is sure to produce problems. In fact, work *is* about problems, and problems *are* work.

Therefore, never treat a problem as a *snag,* always treat it as a *staple* instead. A snag is an irritant, something that ideally should not happen. As a basic feature, a staple is something we expect to encounter and deal with. It is just plain smart to look at problems as part of the *functioning* of the complex machine that is work, rather than as pesky *failures* of this or that cog. If you can truly accept problems as the inescapable fact of life that they are, you are on your way to establishing a healthy relationship with work. Furthermore, any problem coming your way at work is both a puzzle to solve and an opportunity to learn. When you give yourself over to solving the problem, you'll want to find out *what the problem can do for you.*

What is your current problem teaching you about your business? Is it telling you something about yourself, about human nature, about life? How can you put to work what you have learned from it? All this makes sense, but it also takes time. This means that you will take full advantage of these learning opportunities to the extent that you are willing to set aside time for thinking in your daily schedule. Life is a game at which thinkers win. Central to Marcus Aurelius philosophy is the notion that our lives are what our thoughts make them. In other words, the attitude with which we will negotiate our daily encounters with life is going to be the top factor in determining its quality.

HOW TO BECOME AND REMAIN POSITIVE

- If you wish to establish or strengthen your positive disposition, make sure that you develop a reasonably high sense of self-worth. Thinking of yourself as an essentially decent, caring, competent, and accomplished person will allow you to feel that you deserve the good things that come your way. It will also make you confident that you can rebound from setbacks.

- Acquaint yourself with some of the massive body of evidence pointing to the advantages of a genuinely positive outlook on life. Martin Seligman's books *Learned Optimism, Authentic Happiness,* and *Flourish* are a good start.

- Be careful that the advantages of positive thinking do not remain limited to just yourself; they need to be shared by everybody you touch with your life. The world becomes a better place when you become better at being in it.

- Monitor your thoughts in the course of your day. If your inner negativism is on the upswing, stop and reframe your concerns in a positive way.

- Draw inspiration from positive thinkers you know. Their company will strengthen your determination to be positive. Keep them close to you, especially if you are still trying positive thinking on for size.

- Make exercising part of your weekly routines. Physical activity is known to improve your mood. Healthful and nutritious meals won't hurt, either.

- If your will to be positive is flagging, keep acting positively. The feeling will follow. Keep smiling and laughing, and soon you will experience contentment.

The following are major health benefits of positive thinking, as selected by the Mayo Clinic staff:

- Increased life span

- Lower rates of depression

- Lower levels of distress

- Greater resistance to the common cold

- Better psychological and physical well-being

- Reduced risk of death from cardiovascular disease

- Better coping skills during hardships and times of stress

THE WOES OF WORRYING

Thinking at its best is a journey—it successfully takes you from a point of departure to a destination. The destination may be anything, from reaching a new understanding of how the solar system came into being to signing up for ballroom dancing. What does not change is that in good thinking, a healthy sense of self-worth, a rational analysis of situations, and good intuition lead to plausible conclusions and positive actions. While this is obviously the kind of thinking you want to pursue, the kind you want to stay clear of is worrying. Worrying is definitely *not* thinking at its best. Of course, I am not talking about the occasional instance of justified apprehension. I am talking about worrying as an addiction to negativity. In this form, this hybrid of thought and feeling is irrational and unproductive. Rather than a journey with a desirable destination, it brings to mind the nightmarish situation of someone who, stuck in a labyrinth, with undaunted obstinacy keeps choosing the way known to lead nowhere. Serious worrying feeds on cognitive distortions. Among the most common of these anxiety-inducing faulty ways of thinking are:

- Filtering: ignoring the positive aspects in any situation and focusing on the negative ones.

- Overgeneralizing: assuming that what defeated you once will defeat you again and again in the future.

- Catastrophizing: being inclined to expect the worst.

To limit the impact of worrying on your everyday life, you can:

- Train yourself to separate the things you can control from the things you can't. Expel the latter from your conscious mind. In general, be flexible about your expectations.

- Remember that all the turmoil you are experiencing is only in your mind. These thoughts may have hijacked your life, but they are still just thoughts. Changing your life for the better is only as far away as changing your thoughts.

- Keep in mind that very often what you have been worrying about will not happen. When it does happen it generally turns out to be far less daunting and disruptive than expected.

- Force yourself to pay less attention to *how you are feeling* and more to *what you are doing*. Try to remain absorbed in your work for as long as you can. Experiencing the state of flow does marvels for your overall well-being. Since worrying is about the future, it makes sense to minimize its impact by being fully present. Meditation can help.

control is how you *respond* to those events—that is to say, how you *think* about them. Responding positively to something negative is one of the greatest gifts of the human condition. Adversity may strike at any time, but you can bear it better, and even transform it into opportunity, by mustering a positive attitude. True, believing that happiness is a product of the mind means assuming responsibility for it—something we are often reluctant to do. Nevertheless, that positive thinking is a powerful provider of success and happiness has become part of the ethos of our times. The verdict is definitely in: Attitude is destiny.

And then there are relationships. Life is an adventure in relating. We live among others, we depend on others, and we seek comfort in others. Our very identity, sanity, and health are shaped by the presence of others around us. If life is relational, then the quality of our lives must depend on the quality of our relationships. But didn't we just say that happiness depends on attitude? We did, but we must also be realistic. It is not always easy to set our mood to sunny. Sometimes nature, nurture, and circumstance conspire to make us think negative thoughts. Besides, contrary to the opinion of many a philosopher, it may not even be good for us to be totally self-reliant when it comes to the business of thoughts and emotions. It is only natural to look at others as providers of balance and joy. When adversity strikes, by all means look inside yourself for answers. Practice your positive attitude—think good thoughts to the extent that you can. But also seek shelter within the circle of love and support made available to you by your family, friends, and acquaintances.

Although neither attitude nor relationships alone will be enough to guarantee a happy life, together they are a realistic prescription for coping and thriving. Good relationships allow us to be less-than-perfect optimists and stoics. The optimal situation exists when, as they work together, good attitude and good relationships reinforce each other. When we manage to hold on to a good attitude, we are more liked by others; thus our relationships improve and we feel better about ourselves. Improved relationships and feeling better about ourselves will in turn make it easier to maintain our good attitude. Benefiting from this virtuous circle is one of the smartest goals you can set for yourself as you look to direct your increasingly challenging life. When we strip attitude and relationships to their bare essentials, we discover that we are just talking about ourselves and other people. And that is ultimately what we have in life: ourselves and one another. Honoring this elementary truth in our everyday thoughts and actions is the beginning of wisdom and the gateway to happiness.

1. Make a list of the annoying, vexing, or in any way difficult situations over which you have no control that occur with some frequency in your life. Write down how you deal with each of them and evaluate how that works for you.

2. Do the same with the situations over which you do have control.

3. For the next three weeks, keep asking yourself in any problematic situation: "Do I have control over this?" and strive to detach yourself emotionally from situations that you cannot control.

4. Think of a recurring annoyance at home or at work and devise a way of transforming it into an asset.

5. Where does your strength lie, in attitude or in relationships? How can you strengthen your weaker side?

6. Are you the kind of person who worries a lot? For the next three weeks, use the suggestions found in this chapter to lessen the impact of worry on your life. Record your progress in your log or notebook.

8

Being Proactive

PROACTIVITY AS A META-VIRTUE

As you drive in the fast lane of a busy four-lane highway, a sign announcing that your exit is 2.5 miles ahead draws your attention. Although this distance gives you plenty of time to switch lanes, you tell yourself you might as well turn on your right signal immediately. In the next ten seconds, you leisurely cut across one lane of traffic after the other—making sure that you don't cut anybody off—until the time comes for you to take the exit ramp. Had you missed or disregarded the 2.5 miles sign, you might have scrambled to cross lanes at the last moment, creating a safety hazard for yourself and other motorists. By taking the prompt initiative to act, you prevented your situation from needlessly becoming problematic. Doing so was a proactive move. Proactivity is both a dynamic and a wise way of being in the world, often supported by a positive attitude. You are proactive when you are predisposed to intervene as early as possible in any given set of circumstances so that you have the best chances to make them work in your favor. The opposite of the proactive mind is the reactive one, which finds the resolve to act only after problems have taken root and sometimes become intractable. Acting proactively in traffic is certainly smart, but you also want to be proactive in the rest of your everyday life. This will give you an edge in all your endeavors.

"Ten Ways to Be Proactive in Your Personal Life," "Smart Women Live a Proactive Life," "The Proactive Parent's Approach to Teens and Texting," "The Proactive Fund Investor," "The Buddhist Proactive Way," "The Proactive Way to Achieve Happiness": It does not take more than a glance at some of the seventy million Google results for "proactive" to realize that you would search in vain for signs of ambivalence toward the notion on the Net. It is perhaps Stephen Covey's influence that established proactivity as a top virtue of our times. In his iconic book, *The 7 Habits of Highly Effective People,* being proactive becomes more than anticipatory promptness. Enshrined as habit number one, it is presented not just as a staple virtue, but as a sort of meta-virtue, a virtue that makes possible other virtues like self-control. For Covey, being proactive is about being deeply positive, behaving according to values, and taking responsibility for all we do. For Covey, the proactive person is the embodiment of character ethic whose poster hero is Mahatma Gandhi.

PROACTIVITY AS PRUDENCE

One of the outstanding skills you want to become good at is being proactive when it comes to assessing the character of those you encounter in the journey of your life. Most people of good intentions also see the same good intentions in others. As an incentive to connect and relate, this presumption of goodness is certainly an asset, but it can turn into a liability when you do not manage it with caution. Be both open and watchful. Respond in kind to the other person's good qualities without failing to notice personality traits you do not care for. The more you interact, the more data you will collect upon which to base your assessment. A good amount of attention and reflection will go into this exercise in caution, but your investment of time and energy will pay handsome dividends. You will be less likely to suffer the damage that fools unintentionally inflict upon others and less vulnerable to the scheming and manipulating of the ill intentioned. It is your life, you have only one, and it would be somewhat reckless not to be serious about protecting it. Yes, you can always hope to improvise a brilliant solution to a difficult situation. Effective life management, however, is about anticipating that that situation might occur and facing it with a well-thought-out plan. Mistakes are bad choices we make when we are not ready to make good ones. Do think the best of others, but pay attention to evidence, evaluate it, and have the courage to act upon it. This is being proactive, too.

P. M. Forni

THE ART OF BEING PROACTIVE WHEN LEARNING

Strive to be at your physical and mental best at class time through a healthful regimen of nutrition, rest, and exercise (see "Proactive Self-Care," page 99). Build yourself a platform of social support made of acquaintances, fellow students, and friends. In between classes, talk with anybody who appears to be interested in what you are learning. Compare their opinions with yours on issues of wide interest raised by your books. In other words, keep thinking! Do not let any assignment in your syllabus go unstudied. Keep in mind that *reading* is not the same as *studying*. Whereas the effects of the former can be ephemeral, those of the latter are meant to stay with us. Studying is reflecting upon what we are reading to understand and to retain. As you process the material, enter observations and questions into a log that you will then take to class for referral. The more you reflect in between classes, the more sophisticated and rewarding your contributions to class are going to be. Feeling engaged and knowing that you are doing good work, you will see your interest in the subject grow and your ability to pay attention in class grow with it. Make sure you sit in the front of the classroom, where there will be fewer distractions. Turn off all your electronic gadgets and give them a well-deserved, undisturbed rest at the bottom of your knapsack. Now it is your instructor who becomes the focus of your attention. Make occasional eye contact and nod when you understand crucial points. If something puzzles you, wait for a natural pause before asking for clarification.

Remain open to the information coming your way, but look at it through the lens of critical thinking. Is your instructor partial to a methodology and/or an ideology? Are his or her arguments supported by evidence? Your critical stance will strengthen your attention, and your attention will strengthen your critical stance. Refrain from glancing at the computer screen that appears to have totally absorbed the student sitting next to you. Ignore your restless classmates getting up during class discussion to take or make telephone calls in the hall outside. Just remain in your bubble of concentration. Yes, there will be times when your attention will wane and you are about to nod off. The best remedy is acting as though you are interested and alert. If you have been slumping in your chair, sit straight and start being quietly active. Take notes, shift position occasionally, and raise your hand whenever you have a substantial contribution to make. Finally, make sure your whole experience of your class does not revolve around your final grade. If it does, part of the energy you could employ in free, exciting, and even daring intellectual pursuits will be hijacked by your determination to play it safe and please your teacher. Consider your grades not your primary goal, but a by-product of your good work.

THE ART OF BEING PROACTIVE IN A BUSINESS MEETING

You may remember humorist Dave Barry writing, "There are two major kinds of work in the modern corporation or organization:

1. Taking phone messages for people who are in meetings; and
2. Going to meetings." It is true that as a society we spend an extravagant amount of time and energy organizing, attending, and doing follow-ups to untold numbers of meetings at work. Having grown jaded about their effectiveness, many of us participate in the ritual if we must but do so without being able to muster a constructive attitude. Besides not being very professional, this happens not to be very smart. You want to pay attention at meetings because meetings pay attention to you. The meeting you spent exchanging unnecessary messages electronically? Had you paid attention, it would have become clear to you that the new policy up for discussion was very bad for your unit. As it is, you have missed the only opportunity you had to try to persuade your colleagues to postpone its implementation.

It is in part the responsibility of the manager in charge to increase his or her workforce's motivation to be more than just physically present. The meeting needs to be necessary, have a clear agenda, and be kept within the scheduled time limits. Prepare yourself by pondering and annotating the information your manager sent you ahead of it. The more you acquaint yourself with the issues at hand, the more you feel that you are invested in them and the more you will be motivated to pay attention and make your voice heard when the time comes. At the meeting, your posture and eye contact show the presenter and anybody who intervenes that they have your undivided attention. This and taking thoughtful notes will help you fend off the temptation of distraction. Also, make the meeting more interesting by deciding in advance that discussing the items on the agenda is only one reason you are there. The other is that by the time you leave the room, you want to have learned or been reminded of one important thing. It can be something about work or something about life in general. What's important is that the thing be really important. Thanks to this self-imposed goal, you will pay closer attention and ponder the merits of individual insights to select the take-home winner. The overall quality of your experience will increase substantially.

PROACTIVE SELF-CARE

Do you believe that it is your duty to take care of those you love? If you do, then you also have the duty to be proactive when it comes to your own physical health, mental health, and overall well-being. Preventive medicine is a proactive practice. Eat organic and low-fat food, get plenty of rest, see your doctor regularly, exercise, keep your levels of stress down, and look at life as optimistically as you can. You will be alive longer for those close to you. Healthier and more vigorous, you are going to be in a better position to care for them. Chances are that your fitness will have a positive effect on your mood. Since moods are contagious, this is yet another way for your presence to have a positive effect on others. Decreased arguing and fighting will make for a happier you and happier people in your circles of acquaintance and care. In sum, if you take care of yourself, you are more likely to be healthy and happy, and if you are healthy and happy, those around you are sure to benefit in a number of important ways. Trying to remain healthy can be seen as a moral duty, but so can being as happy as you can. Happiness is the ultimate province in the realm of proactivity.

THE BENEFITS OF BEING PROACTIVE

- You are in control of your feelings and therefore of your choices.

- By showing both yourself and the world that you have the willpower to take the path of greater resistance, you increase your sense of self-worth.

- By acting before problems become intractable, you make life less stressful for yourself, your loved ones, and your colleagues.

- By acquiring a reputation as a problem solver, you become indispensable at work and are rewarded with promotions.

- By leading a thinking life, you lead a safer life.

- You are gratified by feeling that you are doing both the right and the expedient thing.

- By promptly taking care of unpleasant tasks, you do not experience the dreading that comes with procrastination.

HOW TO BECOME PROACTIVE

- Sell yourself on the idea. Dozens of good studies document that choosing the proactive way is beneficial to both individuals and organizations. Look for them in publications such as the *Journal of Occupational Health Psychology* and *The Academy of Management Executive*. The more you believe in the efficacy of proactivity, the more likely it is that your effort to make it part of your identity will be successful.

- If you are ready to change your defeating thoughts, engage in simple proactive projects, such as delivering a report well in advance of your deadline so that your boss has plenty of time to integrate it into his or her presentation. Then graduate to more challenging goals such as volunteering for the committee in charge of the yearly high-visibility charitable event sponsored by your organization. Managing to succeed in becoming proactive will require some effort on your part, especially at the beginning. But it will help you believe in yourself.

- Give yourself time to become more proactive without putting too much pressure on yourself. Especially if you are used to procrastinating, it will take you a good amount of time and willpower to get to where you want to be. Stay the course and keep reminding yourself that being proactive really *can* become second nature.

- Keep your levels of attention and curiosity high. Become the kind of person who notices things and immediately thinks how to make them better. Are you the unsung customer of goodwill who takes the time to alert the manager of a restaurant that the lights of the front stairways are out? If you are, hats off to you! An added benefit to routinely being proactive in the small things is that you train yourself to become proactive when it comes to those of greater moment.

- Relationships wilt if you don't nurture them. Keep in touch with the people who are closest to you. Make them feel that it is important for you to have them in your life. Few things matter more than the platforms of social support that we are able to build in the course of our lives. They keep us healthy, sane, and ready to take on the world.

- Keep a record of those you have networked with. Many experts expect our careers to be more fragmented than those of our parents and grandparents. Since transitioning from job to job is already a common occurrence, we are always looking for a job, whether we have one or not. Thus, proactively forging bonds in the world of business is increasingly becoming a way of life. Refer back to your notes when looking for ideas and before meeting again the person in question.

- Education is key. The array of available educational programs, classes, and tutorials is almost overwhelming. Do some research and find out what is out there that fits your interests and goals. It might be a course of study leading to an MBA degree or one giving you online the rudiments of German for business. Maybe what you need to respond to the demands of the market is to attend a webinar on webinars. Keep in mind that besides providing you with usable knowledge, having gone through a good program from a good school looks good on your résumé and can make you more competitive in the job market.

- Willpower transforms proactivity from virtual to real. If you strengthen it, you strengthen your ability to be proactive.

PROACTIVITY AS BEING PREPARED

"I had a friend who was a computer wiz," says Gina, a thirty-something scientist at a multinational chemical company. "One time he hacked into my e-mail account, thinking that it was funny. It obviously was not, and I let him know that I was quite angry. I became very afraid for my privacy, thinking of my e-mails as well as my financial information from online bill payments and passwords for various accounts. I spent weeks setting up a new e-mail account and alerting not only friends and family of the e-mail change, but also my credit card companies, utility services, banks, etc. My friend's reaction was that I was making a mountain out of a molehill and I should relax and forget about the whole thing. He did not seem to realize or care about the havoc his 'joke' had wreaked in my life. I made no mystery of the fact that I considered our friendship ended. Several weeks after he hacked, we were both invited to a party for a very good mutual friend. Since the prospect of running into my hacker former friend gave me a lot of anxiety, I tried to gain some control over the situation by foreshadowing the conversation that would occur. When we met at the party, he was spoiling for a fight with no consideration for the fact that there were other people around. He was loud and profane as he treated me like a whiny child for taking him to task regarding a mere lark. I took a deep breath and calmed myself so that I would not create an uncomfortable scene for any of the other guests and especially the host of the party. This was not the time or place to settle our score. Being prepared, I managed to remain rational, calm, and collected. I think that the people around us were impressed by the fact that I did not lose my cool even though I was repeatedly provoked. They saw strength in my refusing to tussle. He was the one who came across as strident, obnoxious, and boorish. But I do not think I would have pulled this off as well had I not prepared myself for it in advance."

1. What is your definition of proactivity?

2. Report on a few situations you have lived through when proactivity played an important role.

3. Write about a situation in which being proactive benefited not only the proactive person, but others as well. Think, for instance, about the in-flight storing of your carry-on luggage in the overhead compartments. By scrupulously

following the rules about size and weight, you avoid discomfort for other travelers and unpleasant confrontations.

4. According to you, what are the main advantages of going through life with a proactive attitude?

Making Wise Decisions

"THE JUDGMENT OF PARIS"

Mythology loves stories where the heroes reveal what they are made of as their decisions—good or bad—shape their destiny. "The Choice of Hercules," which we encountered in Chapter 4, is one such story. "The Judgment of Paris" is another. Whereas Hercules is able to choose the arduous but ultimately rewarding way of honor and duty, when Paris finds himself at the crucial moment of his life, he shows a different mettle, and his choice will have dire consequences.

The story begins at the wedding of Peleus and Thetis—the future parents of the great Achilles. All the gods of Olympus are invited—that is, with the exception of Eris, goddess of discord. Eris avenges herself in a way consistent with her nature. Appearing uninvited at the festivities, she throws a golden apple on the banquet table brimming with heavenly delicacies. An inscription on the apple reveals that it is intended for the most beautiful among the goddesses present. When trouble inevitably ensues as three of them—Hera, Athena, and Aphrodite—claim the prize, with questionable wisdom Zeus presses into service a mortal as judge of this ultimate beauty contest. This mortal judge of divine beauty is Paris, the son of Priam, king of Troy. As it turns out, however, Paris will be focusing less on how attractive each of the three goddesses is and more on which of the bribes each goddess offers is the most desirable. Hera promises that if he picks her, she will give him a throne from which to rule East and West. For her part, Athena pledges to grant him wisdom and to make him invincible in war. But it is Aphrodite who offers the most appealing gift of all: the love of the most beautiful woman in the world. This woman is the wife of Menelaus, king of Sparta—Helen, whom Paris will eventually abduct to Troy. To restore Helen to her husband and make the Trojans pay for their temerity, the Greeks will assemble the greatest army and fleet ever seen. So as Paris hands the golden apple to Aphrodite, declaring her the most beautiful, he is sealing not only his own destiny (he will die in the war), but that of Troy (which the Greeks will eventually destroy).

This complex myth provides plenty of food for thought:

- When making decisions, nobody is immune from lapses of judgment. The very ruler of Olympus, mighty Zeus, is certainly misguided when he chooses a mortal as the judge in a contest of immortals. "When delegating, double-check credentials" is one possible moral of the story.

- Sometimes accepting a job for which we are not qualified is very tempting. Resist the lure of flattery. Paris has the excuse that his is a command performance and one must say yes to Zeus. You don't have such an excuse.

- One bad decision can lead to another. Having accepted the job, Paris accepts a bribe. In fact, of the three bribes, he accepts the one that immediately appears problematic. His coveted conquest is the wife of a Greek king. This does not bode well.

- A decision that seems to be purely about personal matters can turn out to have an impact on many lives—for better or worse. Paris's choice of love for himself leads to war for the Trojans and Greeks.

- Paris is the anti-Hercules, but both stories remind us that the art of living is the art of choosing. Life tests us all the time. Many tests are of small import, but a few are crucial. Not failing the latter is the secret of the good life.

A LIFE OF CHOICES

"No, no. Look at my tongue," Professor Ciaccia kept saying in between sips of strong black Italian coffee. "My tongue is rolled against my teeth, see? The . . . the . . . the . . . Try it." Try I did, and all of a sudden, it wasn't so difficult after all. "That's better. Keep saying it: the . . . the . . . the . . ." To this day— about fifty years later—I can recall the bittersweet espresso aroma wafting from Professor Ciaccia's bucktoothed mouth as he patiently made sure that I captured the elusive English "th" sound. In the late 1950s, I was a skinny boy of eight or nine, small for my age but showing some promise in school. One day my mother said: "We can't afford both, but you can choose between piano or English lessons."

I'm not sure why I chose English, but I did. Hence my biweekly visits to the home of Professor Ciaccia, a veritable English-language authority in my slumbering northern Italian town. Later, when English came my way as a subject in junior high, I hit the ground running. The language never intimidated me in high school, either, and in my junior year in college, I received a travel grant to visit the United States. A few years later I was studying at UCLA, eventually walking away with a doctorate that allowed me to start my career as a professor in American universities.

I have often wondered if the path that my life took—one so different from those of my childhood friends—was the result of a decision I made without giving it a second thought so many years ago. Would I be writing this book in English now from my home in Baltimore had Professor Ciaccia not made the language familiar to me at such an early age? I doubt it. Would my life have been a happier one had I picked the other option? It is certainly possible that it would have been quite different. What I clearly see when I cast a retrospective glance over my six decades on earth is that who I am today is largely the result of a handful of life-changing decisions I made over the years.

I wish I could tell you that I had the good fortune of undergoing a solid home training in decision making, but I did not. I wish that just one of my teachers had managed to impress upon me and my schoolmates that being happy depends upon making sound choices, that he or she had taught us how to choose well, and that we had gotten it, really gotten it. What a legacy that would have been! Instead, having made my share of bad decisions in my time may be my best credential for giving you advice on how to make good ones. The school of searing regrets is tough but also enlightening if you are willing to listen and reflect. I did listen, and believe me, I reflected. Thus, you will find here the insights without going through the misery yourself. As the proverb goes: "Smart people learn from their mistakes. *Very* smart people learn from other people's mistakes."

Have you ever paused to reflect upon the sheer number and diversity of choices and decisions we are expected to make? From the trivial to the vital, there is virtually no moment of your waking hours when you are not making a choice. Just as you keep breathing, you keep choosing. Will you choose coffee, dessert, or both? Go for the small liberal arts college or the big state university? Recycle scrupulously or not bother? End the date at the door or have unprotected sex? Keep postponing your physical or make the call? Lock your briefcase in the trunk or leave it in full view on the backseat? Tell your spouse he or she hurt your feelings or pretend that nothing happened? Wait for peak hour to pass or plunge into traffic? Step on the brakes or run the red light? Remain a cogwheel of the corporate machine or strike out on your own? Choose your marriage or the bottle? Have an affair or exercise restraint? Each decision counts because it shapes the course of your life, because it opens some possibilities and closes others, and because it can result in added happiness, misery, or both.

Not only can we choose, we can even choose not to choose—only to realize that that is still choosing. Making conscious choices is uniquely human. We see choosing as self-expression, we see it as a quintessential aspect of freedom, and we see it as part of our personal identity. Democratic political systems are festivals of choice, and supermarket aisles offer hard evidence of choice run amok. We keep monitoring the world, saying to ourselves, "This I like . . . this I don't," choosing what to embrace and what to stay away from. And we can choose the attitude with which to confront the world, which ends up being a choice of the kind of life we are going to live.

There is essentially only one way to get in trouble in life, and that is to arrive unprepared at the moments when we must make important decisions. By making right choices in everyday minor incidents, you prepare for when you find yourself at the significant crossroads of life with major decisions to make.

A BAD DECISION

On March 26, 2007, at 3:39 P.M., a red 2005 Jeep Cherokee crossed into the path of oncoming traffic on Sacramento's South Land Park Drive at a speed of about seventy miles per hour. The head-on crash with a slow-moving 1984 Chrysler LeBaron carrying four women and a baby boy on board was catastrophic. Four of the Chrysler's occupants, including the baby, died instantly, and the fifth occupant suffered severe injuries. Surviving with minor injuries was the sixty-four-year-old man at the wheel of the red Jeep. His blood alcohol content was twice the legal limit. According to a police officer testifying at the ensuing trial, in the hours following the tragic collision, the driver had stated that he normally did not drink alcohol, but that day he had "made a bad choice."

Whether it's drinking and driving, pulling the trigger in a lethal robbery, or sexually assaulting and scarring for life an innocent woman, statements such as "I made a bad choice" or "I made a bad decision" seem to have become the standard way for the guilty to rationalize fateful actions.

They are hybrid statements, admitting fault and at the same time subtly exculpating. We may balk at these euphemisms, yet if you think about it, they are accurate. Yes, the choices they refer to are hugely bad ones—choices that drastically change the course of lives for the worse. Hugely bad choices, however, are still choices. An everyday expression such as "I made a bad choice" when applied to events so momentous for both victims and perpetrators sheds light on the crucial role that the act of choosing has in human life.

HOW TO MAKE A GOOD DECISION

This we know for certain: The quality of our lives depends upon the quality of our decision making, and the quality of our decision making depends upon the quality of our thinking. True, our lives are also shaped by circumstances and events beyond our control—think of totally random adversities. The bottom line, however, is undeniable: All other things being equal, it is the wisdom of our choices that determines the quality of our days.

The crucial question then becomes: "How do we go about choosing well?" That we are seldom trained to do that is the single most egregious failure of our educational system. And so, we are on our own. We wander in the realm of decision making without a reliable map. We muddle through, going the trial-and-error way. We acquire experience by getting hurt. Sometimes we get to put that experience to work, and sometimes the damage done by our inept handling of the situation is beyond remedy. This is clearly a toilsome and costly way of going through life. Although we can't prepare specifically for every single thing that may come our way, there is a wide range of challenges that all of us are likely to face. I cannot imagine anything smarter than making sure that we approach the crossroads of our lives—especially the life-changing ones—well equipped to choose well. Being smart does not necessarily mean improvising a solution to a difficult situation on the spur of the moment. It also means anticipating that that situation might occur and therefore facing it with a well-thought-out plan. The following suggestions will offer you substantial help with all the decisions of consequence you will ever make.

Make your decision conscious. Much of your decision making is not planned. If you are like most people, you are not accustomed to thinking, "Here I am, making a decision that can have substantial consequences on the quality of my life and of the lives of several other people. I want to make sure that it is a wise one." You should, though. One of the simplest and most effective ways to improve the quality of our lives is to increase the number of our conscious decisions. Be aware that you are making a decision, remind yourself that it is important that you decide wisely, and budget an amount of thinking time that reflects the importance of the decision at hand.

Gather as much information as you can. Investigate both your current situation and where eventually you want to be by virtue of your decision. This will increase your confidence in your commitment. Gaining a clear sense of the possible consequences of your decision is an important part of your decision making.

Make a list of possible options. Try not to rule out any reasonable ones. Evaluate each of them with regard to your principles, reviewing the impact that each would have on you and on others. Choose the two options with which you are more comfortable. This does not mean the easiest ones; in fact, make sure that you do not rule out good options just because they would inconvenience or embarrass you.

Pick one of two options. Between the two options still on the table, pick the one that seems to dovetail more harmoniously with your plans for your immediate and even long-range future. Should you have doubts about your choice, do a pros and cons evaluation, and if the cons outnumber the pros, go back to the drawing board and start the whole process from scratch again. Maybe there was a flaw in your previous attempt.

Put in place an implementation plan. Think carefully about the possible consequences of your decisions. Do not think in the abstract. Keep constantly in mind the actual configurations of the circumstances in which your decision is going to play out.

All the while:

Think rationally. Do not make an important decision unless you are calm, collected, and ready to evaluate the evidence pro and con. You want to avoid impulsive decisions of the eloping-to-Vegas kind. At work, make decisions that have an intrinsic logic, make sense within the context in which your organization is operating, and do not put excessive strain upon its resources. You want there to still be an organization after your decisions have been implemented.

Think ethically. Your decision should not cause anybody to suffer unfairly. Nor should it make you or anybody else act unlawfully. At work, don't think and act as though the decision were *about* you. It is merely *by* you. The well-being of the organization and not your personal advantage must be paramount in your decision.

Think critically. Question the nature of the information at your disposal and the validity of your own use of it. Are you dealing with verifiable data or with assumptions? Are the inferences in your sources logical and plausible? Are yours? Are you working from different points of view? Don't rely on either intuitive or rational skills alone. A good decision process must avail itself of both.

Think creatively. When appropriate, leave the well-trodden paths of thinking. Look at your decision with the eyes of a stranger with no preconceived notions. This may lead you not just to a good decision, but also to remarkable unrelated insights.

Whenever you are dealing with a difficult decision, review the benefits that your decision will bring to you and others and the negative consequences of not going with it. Seek the support of family and friends. Remember that dreading and stalling are ultimately toxic. Imagine how well you are going to feel after committing to your decision. Take comfort in your conviction that not only is your decision the right one, it is also the right thing to do.

HOW TO CHOOSE BETWEEN TWO OPTIONS

After three days on the road visiting clients, you would love to make it home in time to read to your three-year-old her favorite bedtime story. But the highway sign says you are sixty miles away, fatigue is finally kicking in, and you are fighting an epic battle of wills with your eyelids. Rolling down the window in the hope of making fresh air your ally did not help much, nor did turning up the volume on your XM radio station. You just realized that you have been at the wheel with your eyes closed for the past three or four seconds. Left to its own devices, your car has crept right, half invading the next lane. As you hasten to steady its course, you consider your options. To keep driving is tempting, but to get off the road and rest is the smart choice. Your mind is made up. The next exit ramp is here, and your turn signal is on.

Two goods were in competition. One good was getting home soon, the other was getting home safely. The wiser choice is rather apparent. In fact, given what is at stake here, it is even easier to identify the greater good. If you continue to drive, you could kill yourself or someone else. Yet in a way, it would have been easier to take a chance and keep driving—easier, but not very smart. The easier choice is seldom the right one. Since it is likely to be the path of greater resistance that will lead you to the greater good, plan to rely on your strength of character to stick with your choice.

THE PATH OF GREATER RESISTANCE

Energy is lazy, "energy moves where it is easiest for it to go," organizational consultant Robert Fritz reminds us: "The water in a river flows along the path of least resistance. The wind blowing through the concrete canyons of Manhattan takes the path of least resistance. Electrical currents, whether in simple devices, such as lightbulbs, or in the complex circuitry found in today's sophisticated computers, flow along paths of least resistance." The vital energy of humans works largely the same way. On the campus of the university where I teach, the landscaping is made of straight, intersecting lines. Universities love quadrangles. They also love to put lawns in their quadrangles and believe that grass is a good thing to have there. For many years, our gardeners kept reseeding an area of our quadrangle across from the library where the feet of hundreds of students going to or returning from class day after day carved a bald shortcut in the grassy lawn. But trying to make the students stay on the paved perimeter of the quadrangle proved a losing battle.

So if you come to campus today, you will see among the straight lines of the quadrangle a diagonal, bent, brick-paved pathway crossing the lawn. It is the most recent incarnation of the shortcut that wouldn't go away. The time you save by taking the now officially recognized shortcut: less than twenty seconds. The energy you save: utterly negligible. The only valuable thing it provides is a lesson in human nature. In that bent, brick-paved pathway, we can see the path of lesser resistance materialized. Its existence tells us that when facing two options, humans will always be inclined to choose the one that saves them as much energy as possible and provides them with immediate gratification. Something in us loves a shortcut. So will you take the path of greater resistance or ease into the one of lesser resistance? Both options have in store something good or at least something valuable, but it is the former that usually provides you with a greater good option, the latter with a lesser good option. It cannot be denied that in "The Choice of Hercules" there is something good in the offerings Pleasure has in store for the young hero. Those of Virtue, however, represent a greater good. The problem for all of us arises when the appeal of that lesser good is stronger than the appeal of the greater good. Being able to tell the greater from the lesser good, and then having the fortitude to choose the former over the latter, is the work of the wise. "The Choice of Hercules" demonstrates the importance of intellectual and moral fiber for this physical hero. By resisting the temptations of Pleasure, he shows that his willpower is as strong as his muscles. One moral of this thirteenth labor of Hercules is that sometimes doing the right thing takes a Herculean effort.

A GRAVELLY PATH

It is our penchant for choosing the path of lesser resistance that makes us such good players at procrastination. In this avoidance game, a task comes to us with the option of tackling it now or later. We choose later, trying to put it out of our minds, hoping that "later" will miraculously turn into "never." We are like children pushing unappetizing peas around our plates. At the same time, our truancy preys on us. Somehow, however, inertia still feels better than actually doing what we are supposed to. As time goes by, the task looms larger on our horizon. If we had had the fortitude to choose what appeared to be the more burdensome option (the path of greater resistance, that is), we would have been done with the task long ago. An ironic development of choosing the easy way is that it turns out to be not so easy after all. Escaping the task ignites the dreading, which could be eliminated only by doing, which we are trying so hard to avoid. The moral of the story is to choose the path of greater resistance. It is stony, but you will be in for a pleasant surprise: It becomes much easier on your soles as soon as you start walking on it.

EMOTIONS AND BAD DECISIONS

A seasoned and successful financial consultant, Bill has had plenty of opportunity to observe the role that emotion plays in his clients' decision making. "Emotion," he says, "is much more powerful than facts. It's one of the things that make people who they are. In my experience, you can have all the facts on one side of a ledger that support one thing, but if there is enough emotion on the other side, it's as though those facts don't exist. Every day in my business I deal with two emotions: fear and greed. We all know that in investing we are supposed to 'buy low and sell high.' Why is it, then, that every empirical study proves the same thing, that people do the exact opposite? They buy when they feel good (when prices have gone through the roof) and they sell low (when prices have fallen and people expect that to continue into oblivion). It's not rational, but we all tend to react similarly. And people don't seem to learn from their mistakes. They keep repeating them over and over again. Research proves it! What if we just sat down and thought about the situation before we hit the 'buy' or 'sell' button? What if we relearned to counter fear, greed, and envy with the wisdom of reason, temperance, constancy, and patience? We could become contrarian investors (those who go against the herd) whose success could rival Warren Buffett's!"

ELEANOR'S GOOD DECISION

"I called off a wedding." Eleanor doesn't say "*my* wedding," she says "*a* wedding," as though she needed to distance herself from the very thing for which she is willing to claim full responsibility. A smart pediatric nurse with caring bred in the bone, Eleanor broke her engagement a couple of years ago to an earnest and uncomplicated young man who respected her and looked forward to sharing his life with her. Calling off her wedding was just about the most difficult thing she ever did in her life. By telling her story, she hopes to comfort and inspire people who do not know where to find the strength to make the extremely difficult decisions that deep down in their hearts they know to be the right ones.

So, how did I do it? Well, I think that the "a-ha!" moment was the realization that my feelings mattered. . . . I had long had a nagging feeling that no matter how kind, loving, and just plain nice my fiancé was, we didn't have enough common interests . . . that there was something vital missing from the relationship. A frustrating part of this story was that I saw this and he did not. And, as I mentioned, he was a very nice man, with a nice family, and I had grown to care about them all very much. I did try hard to push my qualms aside. I thought to myself, "You should be grateful to be with someone who doesn't hit you, is nice to you, etc." When the wedding was far away, this sort of thinking worked. I was able to stay in denial. As the wedding approached and things became more concrete, I started to panic. When I was still, the nagging voice in my head started getting louder. Also, I was oversleeping and didn't have the energy to do the things that should've been a really good time. I didn't want to register for gifts, send out the invitations, etc. At last, I started talking about it. I talked with my pastor and with a few select friends. Saying things out loud helped me to realize that I knew what I needed to do—to call things off.

For me, once I acknowledged how I really felt, going ahead with the wedding would have caused such dissonance that I would have been constantly uncomfortable in my own skin. At this point, not to share all this with my fiancé felt like lying. I remember worrying over when was the best time to tell him (there really isn't one) . . . and then ended up telling him the next time we were alone. I couldn't keep back the truth. Although it was hurtful to him, and to me, I was able to tell him because I looked at the bigger picture. Going ahead with things now would only lead to more pain and suffering in the long run—a high potential for divorce, also if we had kids, etc. I was able to make this challenging decision because I care about myself and what is best for me, and also because I care about others and don't want to cause them harm. Also, I came to recognize that I wasn't saying that my fiancé was a bad person—just that he was wrong for me. Someone can be very nice and still not be the right match. And a decision can be the right one and still be very hard.

I am happy to say that the more time goes by, the more convinced I am that I made the right decision. Initially I felt terrible. It was traumatic to undergo so much change, and I did hurt some people that I cared about. I remember desperately wishing that I had a crystal ball that would let me know that I had made the right decision. I also remember thinking that if it was the right decision, I would feel only happiness after making it. . . . Of course, this was not so. And I had to stick with it and let the emotions play themselves out so that I could see how this new life actually felt. There was, to be sure, a sense of relief. This grew stronger over time—and eventually the good feelings and confidence in my decision supplanted the sadness and upheaval involved with making it. I had to grieve the loss of my imagined wedding and marriage—because I didn't stop wanting to be married, only realized that I had not yet found the right person. By letting go of this wrong match, I created for myself the possibility of finding the right one.

What is it that allowed Eleanor to close a painful chapter in her life, minimizing damages present and future? First, relentless introspection; second, a healthy sense of self-worth; and third, enough willpower to capitalize on the first two. Looking inside herself, she acquired essential self-knowledge, which made her aware of what was wrong in her relationship and dwell on the alternatives at her disposal. Her sense of self-worth was crucial because it told her that her feelings mattered and ultimately that *she* mattered. To deliver yourself from misery, it is not enough to acknowledge that misery has you in its clutches; you also need to see yourself as worth being rescued. Finally, Eleanor's willpower enabled her to act upon what she had come to realize was the best decision for herself and her fiancé. Note to self: Be true to self.

1. Make a list of the five most important decisions you made in the past. How did they shape your life?

2. Make a list of five important decisions you may make in the future. What are their possible repercussions on your life?

3. In most circumstances the wise choice is the path of greater resistance, and it is unlikely that you will choose it with any consistency if you have not conditioned your willpower to do so. Presuming you will decide well without first fortifying your character is a reliable predictor of bitter disappointment. Make a list of the things that you dread doing and do them, crossing off the items on the list as you go. Whenever you face an unappealing task, make the effort to tackle it ahead of an appealing one that is also awaiting you. Do not become cozy with dread. Get it out of the picture.

4. Somebody said that life is the art of drawing without an eraser. True, once something has happened we cannot make it un-happen. However, an eraser of sorts comes standard as part of our human condition, and that is our ability to think. This precious tool will not delete our mistakes when we have made them, but it does keep us from making them when we are smart enough to put it to good use. Write down your next important decision, whatever it might be: quitting smoking, taking a job that entails relocating, starting a family, and so on. First imagine making it and then using the eraser and not making it. What are the consequences of each action?

Nurturing Outstanding Thinking: Insight, Discovery, and Creativity

CHARLES DARWIN WAS RIDING ON A LONDON BUS-TOP WHEN SOME KEY THOUGHTS OF HIS THEORY OF EVOLUTION BURST UPON HIM. THIS DOESN'T MEAN THAT THERE IS SOMETHING ABOUT THE TOPSIDE OF A LONDON OMNIBUS THAT TRIGGERS PROFOUND IDEAS ON THE ORIGIN OF THE SPECIES. WHAT IT DOES MEAN IS THAT DARWIN HAD ALLOWED HIS MIND TO FILL UP WITH A COMPLEX PROBLEM UNTIL IT SPILLED OVER INTO THE SUBCONSCIOUS. THE RESULT WAS THAT, EVEN WHEN HE DID NOT CONSCIOUSLY DIRECT HIS THOUGHTS, HIS MIND KEPT WORKING AWAY AT THE PROBLEM, SORTING ALL THE FACTORS THAT WERE BEING ACCUMULATED, WEIGHING THEM, MAKING CONNECTIONS, AND ENGAGING IN ALL THE OPERATIONS LEADING TO A DEDUCTION OR A DISCOVERY. IT WAS THE GESTATIVE PROCESS OF IDEAS, RATHER THAN THE ENVIRONMENT OF A BUS-TOP, THAT WAS RESPONSIBLE FOR THE FLASH THAT ELECTRIFIED DARWIN.

—Norman Cousins

BEFORE "EUREKA!"

For our purposes, "outstanding thinking" will include here "creative thinking," "thinking outside the box," and "lateral thinking," referring to highly valuable cognitive work that stands out by taking place without the safe boundaries of the thinking norm. Outstanding thinking is original and inventive, and sometimes it reshapes a whole field of endeavor.

When Hieron, ruler of Syracuse, suspects that the goldsmith who has made a gold crown for him may have stolen part of the precious metal, he gives Syracuse's resident scientist and philosopher Archimedes (c. 287–c. 212 BCE) the task of establishing whether an inferior metal is present in the crown. It is a daunting task, for he is not allowed to damage the crown in the process. Archimedes knows, of course, that if he manages to find the crown's volume, everything else will be a matter of straightforward calculation. He will divide the weight of the object by its volume, thus obtaining its density, which he will then compare with the known density of unalloyed gold. The wrinkle here is that a crown is not your regular solid that lends itself to easy measurement. How in the world is he supposed to determine its volume? Maybe to take his mind off an apparently unsolvable problem, one day Archimedes decides to take a bath. As he steps into the tub, he is struck by the sight of the rising water. Realizing that the volume of water displaced in the tub must equal the volume of his immersed body, he knows that the crown problem is solved as well. And this is when he bursts out in joy, running naked through the town crying, "Eureka!"—"I found it!" The story is well-known, but I wouldn't be surprised if you told me that the details of its premise with the king, the goldsmith, and the crown are new to you. Accounts of discovery often focus on the exciting moment of insight and almost ignore the hard work of the mind that preceded it. We flatten mercilessly what in reality is a lengthy and complex process. This simplified version then travels through space and time in the form of legend or anecdote.

NEWTON'S APPLE

This is exactly what happened to Sir Isaac Newton's intuition of universal gravitation. In the popular version, one moment Newton is observing an apple fall from its tree, and the next he has figured out that the force that binds all celestial bodies holds the universe together. One moment there is the darkness of ignorance, the next the light of knowledge pours in. "Nature and Nature's laws lay hid in night / God said, *Let Newton be!* And all was *Light*." Even Alexander Pope's brilliant couplet ends up promoting the neat, simplified cause-and-effect way of thinking about the discovery.

In reality, when the obliging apple falls at Woolsthorpe Manor sometime in 1665 or 1666, Newton is already an accomplished scientist. It is the thinking of a lifetime culminating with a Cambridge education that allows his genius to extract such a momentous meaning from the mundane occurrence of an apple falling to the ground. Both Archimedes's and Sir Isaac Newton's are Eureka! moments.

Archimedes found the solution to the problem Hieron gave him. Newton, too, in his own way found what he was looking for. Would Archimedes have made his discovery had he been an uneducated citizen of Syracuse or had he not been pondering the crown conundrum? Would Sir Isaac Newton have discovered the laws of gravity had his mind not been trained by long years of reflection? They would not. The rising water and the falling apple were the necessary conditions for those magnificent insights to happen, but they hardly caused them outright. They were mere catalysts. "In the field of observation, chance favors the prepared mind," said Louis Pasteur. Whether you have the mind of an Archimedes or you are creative on a smaller scale, you cannot achieve your goals without preparing your mind for the job. Where does discovery come from? More often than not, discovery is a flash of intuition made possible by previous untold amounts of reflective thinking.

THE MILLION-DOLLAR PEN

As the story goes, in the 1960s at the time of the space race with Russia, NASA spent millions developing a ballpoint pen. Ordinary pens are of no use in space because they need gravity to convey ink to paper; hence the need for this sophisticated and expensive writing tool. How did the Russians solve the problem? They gave their cosmonauts ordinary pencils. So the Russians won the battle of public relations and the Americans ended up with egg on their faces. The story has been around for a long time and now lives on the Net. It is a good story. It is also an apocryphal one. The Space Pen was indeed researched and developed—not by a governmental agency, however, but by a private corporation, the Fisher Space Pen Company, and no taxpayer money was used. Pencils were not an option because their tips break, which is an obvious hazard in a zero-gravity environment. In the late 1960s, both NASA and the Soviet space agency ended up ordering Fisher Space Pens at a price of $2.39 per pen. Being apocryphal does not prevent the story from being useful as an excellent example of outstanding thinking. The story is about not limiting oneself by remaining mentally on the road more traveled. To come up with a brilliant alternative, one must stop being conditioned by tunnel-vision allegiance to the ostensible task at hand. A willingness to stray is essential. Now the question is not "How do I make a better pen?" but rather "How can one write in space?" and therefore "Is there something better than a pen?" This makes possible the simple and elegant answer: "For my purposes, a pencil is better than a pen."

THE FOSBURY FLOP

There is hardly a better example of taking the road less traveled than the perfecting of the jumping method that ended up revolutionizing the track and field event of the high jump. In the early 1960s, Dick Fosbury was a high-school high jumper in Medford, Oregon, who like everybody else used the leaping-forward "straddle" method—one he felt was ill suited to his physical characteristics. Failing to excel, he started to experiment with a new, counterintuitive leaping-backward method. His coaches tried to dissuade him, but undeterred, he perfected his technique, winning the 1968 National College Athletic Association indoor and outdoor high-jump titles. At the 1968 Summer Olympic Games in Mexico City, the twenty-one-year-old high jumper from Oregon awed the world. Richard Douglas Fosbury did this not by clearing the height of 2.24 meters, which set an Olympic record but fell short of the world one. Rather, it was the way he went about it. After taking a few deliberate strides toward the bar, in a truly astonishing move he turned, leapt off his outside foot, and threw himself backward over the bar, arching his back and landing on it after carefully pulling his legs up and over. It may not have been the most conventionally elegant display of athleticism, but the Fosbury Flop stood the athletic event on its head. Four years later, at the Munich Olympics, twenty-eight out of forty competitors used the flop. To this day, it is the uncontested benchmark high-jumping method. At the 2008 Beijing Olympic Games, it was the method of choice of all competing high jumpers.

THE ELMS AT
BLUNDERSTONE ROOKERY

They are poets and painters, sculptors and novelists, musicians and dancers. Although they may differ in their choice of artistic medium, they are all artists and as such likely to think and express themselves in innovative and imaginative ways. The artist violates the rules of the ordinary grammar of vision. Midway through the first chapter of Charles Dickens's *David Copperfield,* the attentive reader is bound to stop and relish one of the most memorable images in the eminent Victorian's entire work. The passage depicts a corner of the garden at Blunderstone Rookery—the Copperfield estate—on the day of David's birth:

> The evening wind made such a disturbance just now, among some tall old elm-trees at the bottom of the garden, that neither my mother nor Miss Betsey could forbear glancing that way. As the elms bent to one another, like giants who were whispering secrets, and after a few seconds of such repose, fell into a violent flurry, tossing their wild arms about, as if their late confidences were really too wicked for their peace of mind, some weather-beaten ragged old rooks'- nests burdening their higher branches, swung like wrecks upon a stormy sea.

What has Dickens done? He has taken the familiar and unremarkable sight of trees swaying in the wind and transformed it into a mesmerizing and memorable object of beauty. Most of us would barely notice actual trees in real life, yet we stop in awed contemplation of these perturbed arboreal giants. But why are the elms perturbed? What confidences are they sharing that are too disturbing to contemplate? This is where we are tempted to become imaginative in the author's wake. Do they recoil in distress because of the sorrows they foresee the soon-to-be-born David will have to endure? Do the rooks' nests perilously swinging on their branches allude to the young fatherless protagonist growing up without the support of a stable family? Perhaps. What matters is that the author's imagination made our own soar in its wake. This enriched our aesthetic experience of the text.

PAVING THE WAY TO EUREKA!

In their book *Out of the Labyrinth,* Robert and Ellen Kaplan reflect upon whether people can be taught how to have insights. "Suffice it for now to say that insights can be *prepared for* by encouraging an imagination playful to the point of recklessness along with a sort of experimental fervor that follows hypothesis out as if it were truth—but lets it go once revealed as error. It also helps to cultivate a healthy distrust of authority, and a restless, ranging curiosity—not so much an anarchic spirit as the flexible feel for law that tricksters (in the tradition of Odysseus) have." To paraphrase Robert and Ellen Kaplan's question: Can people be taught to become outstanding thinkers? Most of us—perhaps all of us—are potentially capable of outstanding thinking. Not many of us, however, are prepared for it. We have not been trained for it, we are intimidated by it, and sometimes we are not even aware that it is an option. Following are a number of suggestions on taking your first steps in this fascinating field of endeavor.

- Believe in yourself and in your cognitive and creative abilities.

- Start looking at innovations in all sorts of fields and studying the process from idea to realization that brought them into being.

- Keep paying attention to the world around you. Do not take it for granted, but rather develop the habit of questioning what you see and identifying needs and problems to which you can apply your creative skills. Be partial to projects that would solve a problem that is relevant to you. This will keep you motivated. However, you do not need to create something completely new. You can be creative by making better something that already exists.

- Ask "Why?" And when you have your answer, address it with another "Why?" See where continuing to ask "Why?" leads you. "Why?" is your best friend until "How?" enters the picture and you visualize a reality transformed by your intervention and the ways of making that transformation possible, including the apparently impractical and daring ones.

- Fill your pockets with written questions and observations of all kinds collected during the day. Empty them every night, and every few days sort out your notes. Chances are you will find interesting connections among them. This may lead you to insight.

- Connecting things that are far apart from one another allows brilliant people to widen and deepen knowledge and to solve problems. That is what they do. They are in the business of connections.

- Keep your curiosity and enthusiasm alive and healthy. Accept that the complexity of the world may not yield answers as promptly as you would like. As Gary A. Davis observed, "Because most ideas evolve through a series of modifications, approximations, and improvements, creators must cope with uncertainty." Stay with the problem even when there seems to be no solution in sight.

- Flexibility is the handmaiden of creativity. Rely on objective data, but trust your intuition as well. Remain serious about your goals, but let yourself have fun along the way. Changing your daily routines (for instance, going shopping in a different part of town) may bring new stimuli to creativity. Open yourself to new ideas. Be amenable to looking at a problem from more than one point of view and exploring several ways of reaching a solution.

- Choose a congenial spot or an activity that can help you ease into reflection. You may feel comfortable in the anonymity of a busy chain coffee and latte place or prefer communing with nature at the wood picnic table in the park near home when nobody is around. You may be partial to the walk-and-think formula or even the run-and-think one. Try out your different alternatives before choosing the one that works for you.

- Remember that even a small reallocation of time from the pursuit of the digital trivial to the pursuit of outstanding thinking could have momentous repercussions on the quality of your life.

In our ever more complex and vexing world, we need increasing amounts of outstanding thinking to solve our problems and to chart our future. Think what could result from a national effort to make outstanding thinking a school subject. The sooner our representatives in the chambers of power start to consider the nation's thinking needs, the sooner we will be able to look at our future with a renewed and fully justified sense of hope.

1. When was the last time you engaged in outstanding thinking? What was the object of your thoughts? In what way was that thinking creative or outside the box?

2. Do you have plans to develop your creative thinking abilities? What would you like to accomplish with your creative thinking?

3. Choose an outstanding thinker's invention and follow closely the development phases from original idea to finished product. The finished product can be anything that qualifies as the result of creativity: a gadget, a book, a style, a work of art . . .

11

Managing Adversity

AVERTING OUR EYES
FROM ADVERSITY

Adversity is something that happens to others—until it happens to us. When we are in the prime of our lives and eager to prove that we can take on the world, adversity is not what we expect, and even in later years we often feel immune from its ravages. The problem is that living through the good times as though adversity did not exist makes for a traumatic wake-up call when it's our turn to face it. Everything was going as it was supposed to, and now, as our world is turned upside down, we feel like the victims of an unfair deal. Even if we leave it unspoken, the "Why me?" question is never far from our minds.

Prepare for adversity by becoming aware of the misfortunes

of others. Let empathy be your guide as you look at the little girl on the billboard of your local pediatric cancer center—her pretty face swollen by the steroids that barely keep her alive. Why her? Why any of us? The simple reason is that adversity is not an aberration but part of the fabric of life. What you demystify and learn to expect will be easier to withstand. Find out if one or two friends who have dealt effectively with painful setbacks wouldn't mind sharing some of their experiences with you. Some people are not inclined to revisit their painful past. Others feel validated by the request and cherish the opportunity. If your friends are amenable, proceed tactfully and ask just a few important questions: What was the most difficult thing they had to endure? What helped them most? Is there something that they wish they had done differently?

Those you love—your spouse, your child, your friend—are not only precious but also vulnerable. In fact, being vulnerable is in part what makes them precious. There is nothing gruesome or morbid in contemplating what it would be like to lose someone you love. It is in fact a sane exercise that prepares you to face what nobody wants to. If the loss occurs, take the time to grieve, but do not let that be your focus. You want to come to terms with your loss so that you are not deprived of your future. Consider—the Roman Stoic Seneca would say—that for some time she did share your earthly journey. The point is not that she died, but that she lived, and now since you are still alive you want to move on. She wouldn't want to see you trapped in hopeless mourning.

WHAT IS IN OUR CONTROL AND WHAT IS NOT

The Stoics believed that there is a divine design to the universe and that what takes place in it—including the vicissitudes of our own lives—depends on fate. All the things that happen to us, and that we look at as either good or bad, cannot "not happen." But if that is the case, then the rational attitude to adopt in every circumstance of life is to accept with the same tranquillity both the good and the bad. Thus, adversity becomes an opportunity to show that we know how to live wisely, which means deploying our best internal resources—the philosophers in these pages would call them virtues—to face the challenges of the external world.

Slim in size but rich in insight, Epictetus's self-help manual—the *Enchiridion*—remains one of the most influential sources of wisdom that Greco-Roman philosophy bequeathed us. Yet the distracted or hasty reader may never proceed past the book's opening, very plain, and seemingly banal sentence: "Some things are under our control, while others are not under our control." But when we do keep reading, that sentence may strike us retrospectively with the impact of a genuine revelation. Epictetus guides us to ponder that a sizable amount of our soul's turmoil comes from our constant attempts at controlling what we can't. We live within our bodies as though they were invulnerable, and when we get sick we cry foul. With undaunted obstinacy, we develop unhealthy attachments to money or other earthly possessions that can be taken from us at any moment. Predictably, when they are, we feel miserable. By not etching with absolute clarity in our minds that there are things we control and things we do not, we become the providers of our own misery.

Suppose that an unscrupulous business competitor of yours is intent on ruining your reputation among your best clients, and before you even realize what is happening, he or she does you substantial damage. You are understandably upset, but Epictetus would point out that what others say about you is not in your control. What you do have control over is how to respond to what happened, and the wise way to do that is with as much detachment as you can muster. This does not necessarily mean that you should not sue your competitor for defamation of character if you wish. What it does mean is that you can do that from an effective position of serenity and equanimity. These things just happen, and we have no control over the fact that they do. Why fight what has already defeated you? It is by accepting defeat that you come up a winner. Epictetus upends the commonplace manner of thinking about the pursuit of peace of mind. Whereas it is lack of control over human things that usually causes us anxiety, he maintains that it is absurd to be anxious over a thing you can't control. Emotionally detaching yourself from this whole category of things is part—and not a paltry one—of wisdom. Whether it's the loss of your job, a serious illness, the end of an important relationship, or the death of someone very close to you, when the adverse event does happen, don't fight it. It is already part of your life, and it will forever be so.

Although you can almost always find something good in a situation that you would not have chosen for yourself, there is no denying that when adversity strikes, your life is thrown off balance. In many cases, to keep mourning that loss and fighting to return to the status quo is not your best option. The circumstances that allowed your previous existential balance to exist are gone, and they may never return. The smart thing to do is ask, "How can I find a new balance that, although different from the one I lost, still works for me?"

LOSING YOUR JOB

As in all other circumstances in life, when you live through adversity the quality of your life will depend on the nature of your thoughts. You may perceive your plight as a quagmire with no escape, or you can think of it as your gateway to a future better than your present. I do not mean to romanticize one of the most dreadful and stressful events we can experience. There is no denying, however, that as harrowing as it can be, losing your job presents you with the opportunity to do things you usually have no time or inclination for. One of these things is serious thinking. This is the time to take stock of your life, to explore new professional options more in harmony with the person you are today, and, if necessary, to reinvent yourself and your future altogether. This can take the sting out of your forced sabbatical. In fact, you may find the experience liberating—a true spiritual renewal.

"Wait a minute! With a mortgage to pay and a family to feed, you want me to bother with spiritual renewal? I need a job, and at this point I'll take just about any job," a number of my readers will say. Financial obligations don't have to mean that as you search for a job you stop planning your ideal future. Perhaps you can find a stopgap bill-paying job. If so, you also want to prepare yourself for a better one. What is that job going to be like? How can you make yourself competitive for it? You want to be proactive, and to be proactive you need to think.

Adversity allows you to rediscover the importance of what is priceless, such as family, friends, and health. It can even teach you that most difficult of arts: being present in the moment. All you need is the flexibility to revise your priorities. Flexibility, acceptance, optimism, patience, and your commitment to causes larger than your own self-interest are the foundations upon which to build your response to adversity. Don't discount your sense of humor. To all of these strengths, you may be fortunate enough to add faith. Finally, do not underestimate the benefits you may discover from talking about your experience with adversity. Consider every possible format: one-on-one with a friend, a support group, a therapist. You probably could make use of at least two of these options. You may also find it beneficial to write about your time of adversity. Keep a diary or write letters to yourself to make sense of your daily challenges. There is little doubt that talking and writing can provide you with steady comfort. It is also possible that you will find in them the breakthroughs you are looking for.

The great Stoic thinkers remind us that we should accept suffering because it is part of the human condition. We have not completely matured until we have gone through all that comes with adversity. Suffering is always a test. It is a test of our fortitude and resilience when we are the ones who suffer and a test of our compassion when it is others who do. By fostering introspection, adversity fosters self-knowledge and indeed wisdom. Everybody suffers, but it is not everybody's lot to be incapacitated by suffering. We may all be born with different levels of resiliency, but all of us can raise our own. It takes self-awareness and willpower. Maybe there are greater skills in life than finding tranquillity in adversity. Maybe, but if there are, they are not many.

CHRISTIE'S LIST

Craig Toribara was a bright, thoughtful, and handsome seventeen-year-old living in Spokane, Washington. He was a star student and a gifted soccer player. On September 12, 1995, Craig took his own life. In his memory and to make some sense of the tragedy, the Toribaras founded SMILE, an organization dedicated to building resiliency in youngsters with the goal of preventing self-destructive behaviors. Craig's mother, Christie Toribara, is one of the people I admire most. She was kind enough to draw from her harrowing experience and share a detailed set of adversity-related suggestions.

- Live with your adversity. Don't put your life on hold.

- Eat healthily, exercise, take walks, and enjoy the outdoors or places of calm. Do not abuse or overuse drugs or alcohol as a means of numbing the pain.

- Find ways of resting and relaxing, especially when you cannot sleep.

- Allow plenty of grieving time for yourself and those around you. Two people will rarely be at the same level of grief at the same time.

- Be patient with yourself and others. Give yourself time to make decisions without being rash or impulsive.

- Do not feel the need to live up to others' expectations or self-imposed ones. Don't set unrealistic timelines. Be willing to reset goals as you heal.

- Do not feel you must go it alone. Seek professional counseling when needed.

- Be civil in all your interactions. You are not obliged, however, to talk about what could have prevented the painful situation.

- Keep in mind that healing from pain is like a roller-coaster ride. There are times when you are heading up, going down, moving fast, or moving slowly.

- Don't give other people's judgments or manipulative moves unwarranted attention.

- Set your own self-image and goals. Do not allow another's bullying tactics to tear you down or to determine who you are.

- Remove yourself from vicious gossip.

- Don't be afraid not to have a plan; that will come with healing.

- Help others when you feel you are healthy and strong enough. This shifts your focus away from your own pain.

- Pain comes in waves, so give yourself a time-out when you need it.

- Humor is a necessity. Allow yourself to grieve, but at times humor will keep you going. Let the healing power of laughter enter every fiber of your being.

- The most effective way to heal is to reach out with love.

1. What is the adversity that you fear the most? Why do you think it is at the top of your list?

2. If you have experienced adversity in the past at a time when you were not prepared for it, have you done anything in the meantime not to be ambushed by it again?

3. Do you tend not to seek or even to refuse help in difficult times? To what do you attribute this? Is it reserve? Is it

pride? Harold S. Kushner reminds us that a deficient sense of self-worth finds a way of rearing its ugly head even in times of adversity: "One of the worst things that happens to a person who has been hurt by life is that he tends to compound the damage by hurting himself a second time. Not only is he the victim of rejection, bereavement, injury, or bad luck; he often feels the need to see himself as a bad person who had this coming to him, and because of that drives away people who try to come close to him and help him. Too often, in our pain and confusion, we instinctively do the wrong thing. We don't feel that we deserve to be helped, so we let guilt, anger, jealousy, and self-imposed loneliness make a bad situation even worse." Often we are unaware of this inclination that interferes with our ability to enjoy life and to succeed. So take a good look inside yourself. Can you recall a number of instances when you refused to be helped in a moment of need? Did your intransigence take a toll on the people who love you? How would you make the case for letting them help you? Hint: The art of receiving is as important a factor in love as the art of giving.

4. Train yourself in unconditional acceptance. Remember to separate in your mind the things you can control and the things you can't. Eliminating the latter from your horizon of concern won't always be easy, but it is likely that with discipline you can at least manage to detach yourself emotionally from them.

12

Choosing to Be Thoughtful

THOUGHT'FUL, A. 1. FULL OF THOUGHT; MEDITATIVE; THINK-
ING; AS, JOHN WAS QUIET AND THOUGHTFUL.

THOUGHT'FUL, A. 3. HEEDFUL, CAREFUL, ATTENTIVE, ETC.;
ESPECIALLY, CONSIDERATE OF OTHERS; KIND.
—*Webster's New Universal Unabridged Dictionary*

It may happen as you walk down an airport's concourse pulling a wheeled carry-on among innumerable other people doing
the same. All of a sudden, there it is: the unsettling feeling of
being disposable and replaceable. You are just one more face
in an anonymous crowd. It is a humbling thought, which does
not mean that it's necessarily a bad one. It certainly puts things
into perspective. Be that as it may, your mood is not exactly
cheerful.

However, all it takes for you to feel human again is to have a
salesperson rush after you all the way to your gate with the
credit card you inadvertently left in her store. She could have
tossed your card into a drawer and forgotten about it. But she

did not. She treated you as an individual, as a real person, not just another face in a world of billions. She took an interest in you, she put herself in your shoes, and she acted. As she hands you your card with a smile, you can't help basking in this sunny moment of connection. You feel grateful, but you feel more than that. You feel that the world is still a place where acts of gracious goodness can happen. You take comfort in that and, at least for the day, the cynical part of your soul is nowhere to be found.

THE TWO MEANINGS OF "THOUGHTFUL"

With its two distinct but dovetailing meanings, "thoughtful" is one of the great words of the English language. You are thoughtful if you are a thinker, but you are also thoughtful if you are considerate. To be considerate, you need, first of all, to pay attention to other people and care for them—in other words, you need to *think* about them and their well-being. The word's two meanings become one as they sketch the profile of the kind of person you want in your life: as your spouse, child, colleague, or friend. The thoughtful introduce their new co-workers to key people in the organization, and they take them on a tour of the specialty stores in town. At family reunions, they are the ones speaking to the overweight and quirky cousin nobody pays attention to. As houseguests, they empty the dishwasher, go grocery shopping, and make breakfast for everybody. Ever aware of other drivers, they let at least one waiting car merge ahead of them. If they need to take a cell phone call while in a restaurant, they never fail to step out of the dining room. And when nursing a powerful cold, they stay home from work to keep from spreading it to their co-workers. Sometimes they are also paragons of tact, a notion with a ghost quality about it from lack of use. When was the last time you observed that someone was tactful?

As a weary citizen of this highly imperfect world that the thoughtful are so good at making better, I feel a debt of gratitude toward them. Contrary to what they may think about themselves, their gift to the world *does* make them special and *does* deserve recognition. At a time when we desperately need civility so that we can continue to be recognizably human, we need more thoughtful people to model this behavior for the new generations. Anybody who happens to be in a relatively good frame of mind will on occasion be nice to someone else. You don't have to be a bona fide humanitarian to agree to trade seats on a plane so that a family can sit together. But it *does* take a special person to act intentionally and habitually in ways that are beneficial to others, and to do so without waiting to be asked. This is precisely what the thoughtful do. We seldom think of them as thinkers. We connect them to the work of the heart rather than that of the mind, but a good amount of thinking is involved in their giving. To be of help, they must pay attention to the reality around them, identify needs, listen to the voice of empathy, and figure out the best way to implement an act of kindness.

UNCLE BERNIE'S EXQUISITE RUSE

Helping without wounding the pride of those being helped can be the most challenging part of thoughtfulness, requiring a surplus of reflection and benevolent imagination. In his book *Words That Hurt, Words That Heal,* Rabbi Joseph Telushkin showcases these qualities at their finest, recounting an episode from the life of his beloved uncle Bernie, a lawyer and evidently a remarkable man. Having been asked by Rabbi Telushkin's grandfather to see a poor woman with a legal problem, Bernie received her right away, ahead of two clients already waiting in his office. Utterly bewildered, the woman told Rabbi Telushkin's grandfather about the preferential treatment she had received. Bernie explained that the paying clients "would assume that a very important case had come up, which is why I was seeing this woman on such short notice, and, as a result, they wouldn't feel insulted. But, if I had made this woman wait until I had dealt with all my other clients, she would have felt that I saw her as a charity case, and would have felt humiliated." Now, *that* is tact.

VALIDATORS

The thoughtful take genuine pleasure in making others feel good about themselves. They are validators. Chances are that when they build others up, sooner or later they enjoy some form of reciprocity. People can't help liking those who validate them, and they want to make them part of their lives. This strengthens their platform of social support, a crucial quality-of-life factor. Sometimes it may be just a matter of common and simple attention and restraint, but thoughtfulness always lessens someone's life burden. It can create a bond between two people who do not know each other, or it can strengthen an existing bond. By performing thoughtful acts, friends exchange the message that they are still invested in their friendship and that they wish for it to continue and grow. We inherited the genes of ancestors who banded together and shared their prey at the end of the day's hunt. As human beings, we come into the world with an affiliative neurocircuitry—in other words, our brain is hardwired to make us social. When we are thoughtful, we carry out that genetic task at our very best.

ON THINKING BEFORE SPEAKING

This time-honored practice does not seem to have been flourishing in the last few decades. The phrase *thinking before speaking* conveys a concern for both self and other. If you think before speaking, that means you are keenly aware of the power of words and therefore committed to taking the time and trouble to choose them wisely. You do not want to offend the other person, and you do not want to make a fool of yourself, either. Often, taking only a couple of seconds to think over what you are going to say is one of your best investments of time. We usually forget that when we open our mouths to speak, we have made a decision that may have considerable repercussions down the road. Remaining calm and in control is crucial to your ability to choose your best words. Contrast in your mind what you are *instinctively inclined* to say with what you know you should say, and choose the latter. In many cases, you have the option of expanding your thinking time. Just state that you are not ready to take a position yet. "I'm going to get back to you on that" is a perfectly acceptable statement.

THE CHALLENGE OF THINKING BEFORE SPEAKING — OR TWEETING

Upon arriving in Memphis on a business trip on January 14, 2009, James Andrews unwisely made his impression of the place very public by tweeting the following terse statement: "True confession but I'm in one of those towns where I scratch my head and say 'I would die if I had to live here!'" A rash indictment it might have been, but hardly warranting its turbulent aftermath. This post might have been consigned to oblivion had it not come to the attention of FedEx, the very client Mr. Andrews, an executive at Ketchum Interactive, had come to Memphis to see. FedEx's response was immediate, quietly excoriating, and more preachy than the occasion required. Mr. Andrews was reprimanded for his lack of respect toward both the town and FedEx. He was reminded that FedEx was a major account for his company and informed that FedEx could function very well without Ketchum's services.

An apology on Mr. Andrews's blog followed, pointing out that a tweet did not allow for context and that his words were not to be taken as a sweeping assessment of the whole town. Rather, they were his response to an upsetting encounter with an intolerant Memphis resident. The damage, however, was done. The Net was abuzz with what was becoming a cautionary tale about the risks inherent in the mindless use of social media. Mr. Andrews got in trouble for not being as thoughtful (in both senses of the word) as the circumstances required. He unfairly indicted the whole town of Memphis for the intolerance of one of its residents. And he failed to consider that once recorded and made public on Twitter, his words might come back to haunt him, such being life in the digital age. Only a few months later, Mr. Andrews quit his position as vice president at Ketchum to found his own consulting company.

I often speak to medical organizations about the costs—in terms of both human misery and dollars—of uncivil workplace behavior. A frequent segment of my presentations is a narrative I conveniently crafted to make my point. Although it is not a true story, it could be, based as it is upon known disruptive dynamics of interaction and their consequences in the medical workplace. Something along its lines has happened untold times in hospitals around the world. In fact, something similar is probably happening somewhere at this very moment. Here is the story of Dr. X, Dr. Y, and the ripple effect of the failure to think before speaking.

When Dr. Y, one of Dr. X's young interns, neglects to execute a scheduled procedure on a noncritical patient, Dr. X's angry outburst right in front of three patients, A, B, and C, and a couple of nurses raises a few eyebrows. Sins of omission are not a trifling matter in health care, but this one was not the end of the world, either. Dr. X's reaction seems excessive and ill timed to Dr. X himself, who immediately regrets not having stopped to think before upbraiding his young colleague so harshly. The damage is done, but what exactly does it consist of? Patient A begins to doubt Dr. Y's competence. Maybe he deserves to be treated in such a demeaning way because he is not a good doctor, Patient A thinks. Patient B is struck instead by the fact that the more experienced Dr. X has shown little consideration to his younger colleague. He should have expressed his displeasure in private. Patient B, for whom a doctor's relational skills are proxies of his clinical skills, begins to wonder whether Dr. X is a good doctor. Patient C has a reaction that goes beyond the two physicians in question: She can't help wondering about the hospital itself. Was she foolish to entrust the care of her health to a place where a patient is treated to such a display of unprofessional behavior? What else might be wrong around here? Her faith in the institution is shaken.

And then there is Patient D, the patient whom young Dr. Y sees minutes after his searing encounter with Dr. X. Dr. Y is so upset that he does not evaluate Patient D properly, thus failing to prescribe the adjustment in medication that his patient needs. Fortunately, a perceptive and competent nurse steps in, and the patient ends up receiving the care he needs. Finally, in the wake of the incident, Dr. Y avoids Dr. X, and the few interactions the two health professionals do have are predictably awkward. Although still a member of Dr. X's team, Dr. Y does not contribute with the intensity of the past. He remains silent at the grand rounds, and he does not ask Dr. X's opinion when handling difficult cases the way he used to. After a few weeks, he is sending his curriculum vitae to several hospitals in the area. By any standards, the incident had a costly set of consequences. Part of the problem is that Dr. X does nothing to make Dr. Y feel that he is still a bona fide member of his team. Would the enactment of a healing ritual of reinclusion with apologies from Dr. X have made the difference? Perhaps. Was Dr. Y a good doctor who needed guidance in order to come into his own? Is the hospital losing a professional who might have become an asset? We may never know.

WHY YOU SHOULD THINK BEFORE SPEAKING

Here are five main reasons to think before speaking—or e-mailing, posting, tweeting, or texting:

- To make sure you do not let impulse or temper get the best of you. Obviously, by stopping to think, you can avoid saying things that you do not mean and/or are going to regret. Consider the wisdom of what you are about to say. Before actually saying it, think: Is there a better option, something you *should* or *need* to say instead?

- To do justice to what you are discussing and confer respect upon both yourself and others. By showing that your interaction with them is important to you, you will impress people and make them feel validated.

- To give clarity a chance to blossom. You want to put order in your mind and choose the words that best serve what you want to communicate. Part of this is considering the person or persons at the receiving end of your words. By tailoring your message, you will avoid misunderstanding, be more persuasive, and make a more lasting impression.

- To make sure that what you are going to say is appropriate. You can reduce the chances that your words will inadvertently hurt someone's feelings.

- To make sure that when you are ready to speak, you are prepared and poised. There is *gravitas* in pacing yourself. Your contribution to the conversation will be authoritative. People are going to listen to you with real attention. The quality of your interaction will increase as your interlocutors realize your determination to do justice to the issues at hand. Showing that your exchange with them is important to you will make them feel validated.

The process of thinking before speaking often takes only a handful of seconds, making it one of your best investments of time. We are not just talking about letting a trickle of words come out of your mouth. We are talking about your ability to relate to your fellow humans.

WHAT PREVENTS US FROM THINKING BEFORE SPEAKING

Anger, lack of time, lack of self-respect, lack of respect for our interlocutors, excitement, carelessness, fatigue, laziness, and feeling the need to fill the awkward moments of silence in conversations: These are the more frequent factors that contribute to our speaking impulsively. Vanity and narcissism are poor counselors as well. They make us presume that our contribution to the conversation is so important that we must give it at all costs, even if we have not prepared ourselves, even if we have nothing of substance to say. So we give it, and we either utter something negligible or we end up making fools of ourselves.

NEEDLESSLY HURTING WORDS

After her teen son, Craig, committed suicide, Christie Toribara—whom I introduced in Chapter 11—was astounded by the hurtful words uttered by both youngsters and adults at Craig's school and her workplace. Some members of the football team joked that it was okay that Craig died since he was only a soccer player and a musician. On Christie's first day at work following her son's death, a woman rushed up to inform her that families fell apart and parents got divorced after a loss such as the one she had suffered. Someone else blurted out that Craig must have been a drug addict or an alcoholic. After the Toribara family established SMILE, the not-for-profit organization involved in the prevention of teen suicide, a school counselor told Christie: "It is so good that your son died—look how much has come from it!" This cruel statement is a reminder that when it comes to thinking before speaking, we want to stop to consider not only the content but the form of our contribution to the conversation. One can easily imagine a rephrasing of the counselor's statement that would make it perfectly fitting: "Ms. Toribara, I do not presume to know how you cope with this tragedy, but I do hope that you find some comfort in the wonderful work you and SMILE are doing."

Nescit vox missa reverti. "A word once spoken cannot be called back." Horace's famous line is usually evoked in reference to big verbal blunders that we wish we could take back. But this fragment of Latin wisdom remains relevant even for utterances that are not terribly embarrassing. We meet someone for the first time, and after five minutes we realize that everything we have said has been shallow and unfocused, of no interest to the person we have just met or even to ourselves. Why did we not take the time to think before speaking and to choose the right words? (Not fancy words, mind you, just the ones that clarity and precision demand.) This was our opportunity to make a great first impression and we blew it.

We all bring to our way of speaking our identity and our personal history. If we are lacking in self-worth, we believe that our thoughts are not so important. Consequently, we have little motivation to think and convey our thoughts to others. This atrophies our thinking muscles. When we do speak, our perceived inadequacy becomes self-fulfilling. The fear of exposing our mediocrity makes us give a mediocre performance, leaving us unhappy with ourselves and leery about going through the small ordeal again anytime soon. Take time to build your self-esteem, either on your own or with help. Just as there is pitch in singing, so is there nuance in conversation. Hitting the right notes in the latter is as exhilarating as hitting them in the former. When you do so on a regular basis, you can expect to increase your chances to flourish.

L'ESPRIT DE L'ESCALIER

Which is worse, saying the wrong thing or not saying the right one? Would you be more irritated after blurting out something inadequate (or erroneous or embarrassing) or by not finding the words the situation requires? Although in this chapter I am intentionally focusing on the former, I am going to at least acknowledge the latter here. We all have experienced the frustration of finding ourselves speechless at the very moment a clever response is called for. French writer Denis Diderot spoke of an "esprit de l'escalier," or the "wit of the staircase." He meant that smart remarks have a way of coming to us not when they would make us shine, but when the party is over and we are walking down the stairs and on our way home. In *Viva la Repartee,* his wonderful collection of witty retorts from different cultures and times, Mardy Grothe flags one as "perhaps *the* classic example in the history of wit." The anecdote springs from the well-known political rivalry between John Montagu (the Fourth Earl of Sandwich) and reformist John Wilkes. "During a heated argument, Montagu scowled at Wilkes and said derisively, 'Upon my soul, Wilkes, I don't know whether you'll die upon the gallows, or of syphilis.' . . . Unfazed, Wilkes came back with what many people regard as one of the greatest retorts of all time: 'That will depend, my Lord, on whether I embrace your principles, or your mistress.'" That such a brilliantly clever retort could have been conjured up instantly is amazing. But for most of us, being concise and articulate would be good enough under any circumstances.

SELF-TALK — THE WRONG KIND

Although it is certainly honorable to consider the effects that our words have upon others, we should not ignore the effects they have upon ourselves. So many of us are such accomplished spinners of critical self-talk! Are you inclined to find in yourself only shortcomings, mistakes, and failings? Maybe you routinely pronounce unflattering, unquestioned, and unfair judgments against yourself, such as "You can't do anything right," "You are disgustingly fat," "Nobody will ever love you," "You'll never make it." Of course, by *saying* that you will never make it, you *are* already halfway there—halfway to nowhere. Make sure that you don't get bogged down in this kind of negative self-talk. Tell yourself a more flattering narrative of yourself. Look at your accomplishments. Stop and think the best of you.

But if you should slip into the pit of defeatist self-doubt, do not lose a moment. Fight alone or fight with help, but do get out of it.

THE THOUGHTFUL LEADER

When a system of management based on authority breaks down, one based on communication must take its place. We are at precisely such a juncture in history. Although he has not disappeared, the dictator boss of yesteryear is becoming an endangered species. The leader of today is less of an enforcer and more of a first among equals—someone who lets you know *why* something needs to be done and asks for your input as to *how* to do it. There is a new awareness that workers come with personal identities (gender and ethnicity, for instance) that require respect and tending. Managing these new workers includes helping them manage their own work/life continuum.

In part, these developments are a result of the new sensibilities surrounding equality, equity, and diversity that flowered in the wake of the civil rights movement. What matters here, however, is that in a world where the business of leading and managing has become an exercise in inclusion, persuasion, recognition, and an overall attention to the worker as a person, we need new leaders and we need them to be strong communicators. In other words, they need to become proficient in a whole new set of thinking skills. If you are in a leadership position, you know that your co-workers pay a lot of attention to your words, especially in a soft economy, when everybody is concerned about the future. Stopping to think before you speak should be part of your job description and part of who you are. Speak in a candid and straightforward manner. If the situation warrants it, use a vocabulary of optimism and hope—always tempered by realism. A trusted and positive leader forthcoming with information can curb the doomsday rumors that are so detrimental to workforce morale, health, and productivity. Do stop to think, do it frequently, and make sure you perform periodic self-assessments as to how you are faring. Being a thoughtful communicator will make you an invaluable asset— to yourself and to your organization.

A final note. "On each occasion [. . .] a man should ask himself, 'Do I really need to say or to do this?' In this way, he will remove not only unnecessary actions, but also the superfluous ideas that inspire needless acts." Thus, as we saw in Chapter 1, spoke Marcus Aurelius. Make a habit of thinking about the necessity of what you are about to do or say. When it comes to the pursuit of the good life, there is hardly anything more effective than adopting such an existential policy. Ultimately, you want to think before speaking for the same reason that you want to think before taking any action. Since life matters, it deserves to be taken seriously. Whenever you choose to think, you do justice to the importance of life. Thinking before speaking is the right thing to do and the expedient one as well.

1. Which of the two meanings of "thoughtful" applies to you more than the other: "a person who thinks a lot" or "a considerate person"?

2. If being considerate is your forte, how can you improve your overall thinking abilities?

3. If you are someone who thinks a lot, how can you become more considerate?

4. Do you consider yourself a validator? If you do, what makes you so?

5. Do you consider yourself a thoughtful leader? Give a couple of examples of what that means to you.

6. When it comes to thinking before speaking, on a scale from one to ten (ten being the highest level of ability), where would you situate yourself?

Conclusion:
We Are What We Think

TO LIVE IN THE WORLD OF CREATION—TO GET INTO IT AND
STAY IN IT—TO FREQUENT IT AND HAUNT IT—TO *THINK*
INTENSELY AND FRUITFULLY—TO WOO COMBINATIONS AND
INSPIRATIONS INTO BEING BY A DEPTH AND CONTINUITY OF
ATTENTION AND MEDITATION—THIS IS THE ONLY THING. . . .

—*Henry James*

When we go through life unaware of the importance of engaging in serious thinking or unwilling to take the time to do
so, we reduce our chances to be happy. Unfortunately, in the age
of distraction, this is the lot in life of millions (if not billions) of
us. Insufficient and shallow thinking:

- Causes you to botch your relationships with the most
  important people in your life.

- Negatively impacts your effectiveness at work, thus hinder-
  ing your prospects.

- Prevents you from arriving prepared at the crossroads of life, where the decisions you make decide the quality of your future.

- Leaves you at the mercy of adversity, without a proven coping strategy.

- Can endanger your well-being or your very life by keeping you from contemplating the consequences of your actions.

- Makes you unable to understand and cultivate your strengths and therefore interferes with your ability to achieve happiness.

The problem, then, is being smart enough not to get mired in trivialities, thus finding at our disposal the spare time to engage in truly effective thinking. This is the thinking that:

- Makes you aware of other people's needs, which is necessary to having harmonious relationships with them. Empathy is a form of thinking.

- Makes you more productive at work. Great teamwork, sustained focus, creativity, and good leadership are all made possible by outstanding thinking.

- Allows you to be more in charge of your future than you would otherwise be. Being proactive is the decisive factor here.

- Allows you to soften the blow of adverse events large and small. The mental preparation you did in the good times will pay off handsomely.

- Keeps you from suffering the negative consequences of impulsive decisions.

- Enables you to know your weaknesses and how to compensate for them, and your strengths and how to capitalize on them.

This book has given you an alternative to the life wasting of the age of distraction. That alternative is the thinking life, which entails engaging in life fully by placing serious thinking at the center of it. *Life* is a versatile word. With it we refer to the *state* of being alive but also to our *time* on earth. We speak of animal life and we speak of plant life. There is, ultimately, life on earth—all the living organisms on the planet and all that has an impact on . . . well, yes . . . their lives. Whatever we may refer to exactly each time we use the word, one thing does not change: Life matters, life is important. It is from this notion that everything you found in these pages derives its deepest meaning. Perhaps life is important to you because you see it as God's creation. Or from a secular point of view it is both the grief we must endure on earth and the joy that brightens our days to make it a serious matter. Maybe most of us find life precious because the thought that sooner or later it ends is never far from us. We are like visitors to a Renaissance chapel looking at remarkable painted canvases on the walls as the lighting timer we activated ticks away. We enjoy the interval of sweet light allotted to us before the darkness envelops us again. Just as darkness makes light precious, frailty and mortality increase the

value of our time under the sun. If we agree that life is important, then thinking as we go through it is the basic tribute we
owe it. It also happens to be the golden way to the good life—
the kind of life in which happiness blooms.

Notes

INTRODUCTION: THINKING SERIOUSLY ABOUT SERIOUS THINKING

Norman Cousins said: Norman Cousins, *Human Options: An Autobiographical Notebook.* New York: Norton, 1981, p. 28.

"to become happy and to remain so": Sigmund Freud, *Civilization and Its Discontents,* ed. James Strachey. New York: Norton, 1961, p. 23.

"The life which is unexamined": Plato, *Apology* in *Euthyphro Apology Crito Phaedo,* tran. Benjamin Jovett. Amherst, NY: Prometheus Books, 1988, p. 49.

CHAPTER 1: WHY YOU DON'T THINK AND WHY YOU SHOULD

"Is it not better": Marcus Aurelius, *The Emperor's Handbook,* C. Scot Hicks and David V. Hicks, eds. New York: Scribner, 2002, p. 46.

A charming vignette: William Powers, *Hamlet's BlackBerry: A Practical Philosophy for Building a Good Life in the Digital Age.* New York: Harper, 2010, p. 9.

CHAPTER 3: ATTENTION: AWARENESS AND MUCH MORE

William James wrote: William James, *The Principles of Psychology*, Vol. 1. New York: Henry Holt, 1931, pp. 403–404.

"There is no part of the activities": *Discourses,* in Vol. II of Epictetus's works. Cambridge, Mass.: Harvard University Press, 2000, pp. 423–425.

M. Scott Peck powerfully: M. Scott Peck, *The Road Less Traveled: A New Psychology of Love, Traditional Values and Spiritual Growth.* New York: Touchstone, 1979, p. 120.

CHAPTER 5: INTROSPECTION: SELF-KNOWLEDGE FOR SUCCESS

In his influential book: Martin Seligman, *Authentic Happiness: Using the New Positive Psychology to Realize Your Potential for Lasting Fulfillment.* New York: Free Press, 2004.

CHAPTER 6: EXERCISING SELF-CONTROL

Ethicist Joshua Halberstam observed: Joshua Halberstam, *Everyday Ethics: Inspired Solutions to Real-Life Dilemmas.* New York: Penguin, 1994, p. 105.

Adams twice identifies: *The Works of John Adams*, Vol. 9. Boston: Little, Brown and Company, 1865, p. 229.

The real greatness of a nation: Lord Moulton [John Fletcher Moulton], "Law and Manners," *The Atlantic Monthly,* July 1924. N. 1, p. 2.

He dropped all expressions: Benjamin Franklin, *The Autobiography of Benjamin Franklin,* in *Autobiography and Other Writings,* ed. Kenneth Silverman. New York: Penguin, 1986, pp. 18–19.

CHAPTER 7: EMBRACING THE POSITIVE

The following are: Mayo Clinic Staff, "Positive Thinking: Reduce Stress, Enjoy Life More," http://www.mayoclinic.com/health/positive.thinking/ SR00009/ME.

CHAPTER 8: BEING PROACTIVE

It is perhaps Stephen Covey's influence: Stephen R. Covey, *The 7 Habits of Highly Effective People: Restoring the Character Ethic.* New York: Free Press, 1990.

You may remember humorist Dave Barry writing: Dave Barry, *Claw Your Way to the Top: How to Become the Head of a Major Corporation in Roughly a Week.* New York: Rodale, 1986, p. 21.

CHAPTER 9: MAKING WISE DECISIONS

"energy moves where it is easiest for it to go": Robert Fritz, *The Path of Least Resistance: Learning to Become the Creative Force in Your Own Life.* New York: Fawcett Columbine, 1989, p. 4.

Notes

CHAPTER 10: NURTURING OUTSTANDING THINKING: INSIGHT, DISCOVERY, AND CREATIVITY

"Nature and Nature's laws": *The Poems of Alexander Pope*, John Butt, ed. New Haven: Yale University Press, 1963, p. 808.

"The evening wind": Charles Dickens, *David Copperfield.* New York: Bantam, 1981, p. 5.

In their book *Out of the Labyrinth*: Robert Kaplan and Ellen Kaplan, *Out of the Labyrinth: Setting Mathematics Free.* New York: Oxford University Press, 2007, p. 16.

CHAPTER 11: MANAGING ADVERSITY

"Some things are under our control": *Enchiridion,* in Vol. II of Epictetus's works. Cambridge, Mass.: Harvard University Press, 2000, p. 483.

"One of the worst things": Harold S. Kushner, *When Bad Things Happen to Good People.* New York: Anchor, 1989, p. 97.

CHAPTER 12: CHOOSING TO BE THOUGHTFUL

In his book *Words That Hurt*: Joseph Telushkin, *Words That Hurt, Words That Heal: How to Choose Words Wisely and Well.* New York: Harper, 1995, pp. xi–xii.

Mardy Grothe flags: Mardy Grothe, *Viva la Repartee: Clever Comebacks and Witty Retorts from History's Great Wits and Wordsmiths.* New York: Collins, 2005, pp. 3–4.

"**When a system of management**": The observations in this paragraph and the following appeared first in an article published in *One*, the magazine of the Johns Hopkins Carey Business School. "Why Civility Means Business: A Memo to the B-School Dean (cc: the CEO)" appeared in Vol. II, no. 2, Spring/Summer 2010, pp. 6–7.